# Understanding the Danish F
## School Approach

This fully revised edition of *Understanding the Danish Forest School Approach* is a much needed source of information for those wishing to extend and consolidate their understanding of the Danish Forest School Approach. It enables analysis of the essential elements of this particular approach to early childhood teaching and the relationship it holds with quality early years practice.

Describing the key principles of the Forest School Approach to early childhood, and heavily supported with practical examples and case studies, each chapter ends with highlighted key points, followed by reflect-ions on practice to aid discussion and reflection on own practice. Including a new chapter on the curriculum, this text explores all aspects of the approach including:

- The geographical, historical, social and cultural influences that have shaped the philosophy and pedagogy of the early years setting in Denmark.
- The people and theories that have influenced and supported the practices of using the outdoors with children.
- An analysis of the learning environments, their risks and challenges and what a learning environment is made up of.
- The Danish early years curriculum; the areas of learning and the way pedagogues facilitate the learning processes.
- Parental, political and research perspectives on the approach and the sustainability of its future.

*Understanding the Danish Forest School Approach* highlights the key ideas that practitioners should consider when reviewing and reflecting on their own practice, and outlines the national appraisals and evaluations of the curriculum. Providing students and practitioners with key information about a major pedagogical influence on early years practice, this is a vital text for students, early years and childcare practitioners, teachers, early years professionals, children's centre professionals, lecturers, advisory teachers and setting managers.

**Jane Williams-Siegfredsen** is Director and Consultant for Inside-Out Nature, based in Denmark.

## Understanding the… Approach
Series Editors: Pat Brunton and Linda Thornton

This series provides a much needed source of information for those wishing to extend and consolidate their understanding of international approaches to early years education and childcare. The books will enable the reader to analyse the essential elements of each approach and its relationship to quality early years practice.

Each book:

- Describes the key principles of the approach to early childhood with practical examples and case studies.
- Provides students and practitioners with the relevant information about a key pedagogical influence on high-quality early years practice.
- Highlights the key ideas that practitioners should consider when reviewing and reflecting on their own practice.
- Can be used as the basis for continuing professional development and action research.

Written to support the work of all those in the field of early years education and childcare, these will be invaluable texts for students, early years and childcare practitioners, teachers, early years professionals, children's centre professionals, lecturers, advisory teachers, head teachers and setting managers.

Titles in this series:

*Understanding the Montessori Approach*     (978-0-415-58503-3)
**Barbara Isaacs**

*Understanding the HighScope Approach*     (978-0-415-58358-9)
**Monica Wiltshire**

*Understanding the Te Whariki Approach*     (978-0-415-61713-0)
**Wendy Lee, Margaret Carr, Linda Mitchell and Brenda Soutar**

*Understanding the Steiner Waldorf Approach*     (978-0-415-59716-6)
**Janni Nicol and Jill Taplin**

*Understanding the Reggio Approach*     (978-1-138-78438-3)
**Linda Thornton and Pat Brunton**

# Understanding the Danish Forest School Approach

Early Years Education in Practice

Second Edition

Jane Williams-Siegfredsen

Routledge
Taylor & Francis Group

LONDON AND NEW YORK

Second edition published 2017
by Routledge
2 Park Square, Milton Park, Abingdon, Oxon OX14 4RN

and by Routledge
711 Third Avenue, New York, NY 10017

*Routledge is an imprint of the Taylor & Francis Group, an informa business*

First edition published 2011

*British Library Cataloguing in Publication Data*
A catalogue record for this book is available from the British Library

*Library of Congress Cataloging in Publication Data*
Names: Williams-Siegfredsen, Jane, author.
Title: Understanding the Danish Forest School Approach : early years
education in practice / Jane Williams-Siegfredsen.
Description: Second edition. | New York : Routledge, 2017. | "First edition
published 2011"--T.p. verso. | Includes index.
Identifiers: LCCN 2016040968 (print) | LCCN 2016056778 (ebook) | ISBN
9781138688087 (hbk : alk. paper) | ISBN 9781138688094 (pbk : alk. paper) |
ISBN 9781315542027 (ebk)
Subjects: LCSH: Nature--Study and teaching (Early childhood)--Denmark. |
Outdoor education--Denmark.
Classification: LCC LB1139.5.S35 W545 2017 (print) | LCC LB1139.5.S35 (ebook)
| DDC 371.3/8409489--dc23
LC record available at https://lccn.loc.gov/2016040968

ISBN: 978-1-138-68808-7 (hbk)
ISBN: 978-1-138-68809-4 (pbk)
ISBN: 978-1-315-54202-7 (ebk)

Typeset in Palatino
by Fish Books Ltd.

MIX
Paper from
responsible sources
FSC
www.fsc.org    FSC® C013056

Printed and bound in Great Britain by
TJ International Ltd, Padstow, Cornwall

# Dedication

This book is dedicated to Megan and Emily. May you always find wonder in nature.

# Contents

# Contents

# Introduction

In 1993 I was among a group of lecturers from Bridgwater College who took their early years students on a study trip to Denmark; we'd heard about the good practice there and wanted to see for ourselves what made it so good. I remember my first visit to a *skovbørnehave* (forest kindergarten). I was totally bowled over by what I saw – children free to play and roam the wooded area beside their kindergarten. The children were confident and competent in their play, climbing trees and imaginatively making up games using the natural materials around them, and although there was a language barrier, they took delight in showing their skills and knowledge. I remember seeing a child high up in one of the trees and I called to a pedagogue close by, 'there's a child high in the tree'; the pedagogue replied, 'yes there is'. Horrified, I said, 'but they may fall out!', 'Yes' said the pedagogue, 'they might, but they don't usually!' At first I thought about how the pedagogues could allow children to take such risks and why they seemed so unconcerned that an accident might happen. Now, 18 years later, I understand why; children need to start to develop their physical skills and agility at an early age and alongside that, with the support and encouragement from the pedagogues, develop their understanding of how to assess risks and challenges. Children generally do not climb higher than they feel comfortable with and do not like pain and fear.

After the study trip a 'Forest School' was started for Bridgwater College's children's centre; the concept spread and there are now Forest Schools in many parts of the UK. The term 'Forest School' was a made-up English name for what we had seen in Denmark. There are no 'Forest Schools' as such in Denmark – what you will read about in this book are *skovbørnehaver* (forest kindergartens), *skovegrupper* (forest or wood groups), *naturbørnehaver* (nature kindergartens) and ordinary early years settings that use the outdoor area they have available.

I moved to Denmark in 1997 and have the pleasure and privilege now to spend my time working with a number of early years settings – some are in the forest and others in the town, but all use their outdoor area and nature every day, all year round.

The interest in what happens here in Denmark is still growing; on the residential courses I arrange here there have been participants from all over the UK, Portugal, the USA, Canada, Australia, Greece, China and Spain. I have regular email contact with people worldwide wanting to know more about Danish pedagogy and early years practice.

## Structure of the book

Chapter One describes the geographical, historical, social and cultural influences that have shaped the philosophy and pedagogy of the early years setting in Denmark and in particular the Danish Forest School Approach.

Chapter Two looks at the people and theories that have influenced and supported the practices of using the outdoors with children and gives examples of present-day practice supporting the theories.

Chapter Three describes the history and training of Danish pedagogues and looks at their roles in early years settings.

Chapter Four investigates the learning environment and what constitutes a learning environment. In this chapter practical examples from Danish early years settings are given to illustrate the theory and practice of understanding learning environments. Risk and challenge is also discussed here and the need for children to be able to assess risks for themselves.

Chapter Five looks at the Danish early years curriculum, the areas of learning and the way pedagogues facilitate the learning processes. Connections between the early years curriculum and sensory development are discussed. In the final part of the chapter, the national appraisals and evaluations of the curriculum are outlined.

Chapter Six describes the organisation and layout of settings and uses three examples of kindergartens to illustrate practices.

Chapter Seven considers the future of the Danish Forest School Approach. Parental, political and research perspectives indicate a trend towards a growth of interest in the Approach and the sustainability of its future.

A glossary of terms used in the book is also provided to explain the pedagogical and Danish terms used.

Please note that in the text 'pedagogue' is used when describing the people working with children in Denmark and 'practitioner' is used when referring to those working with children in other countries.

## Structure of the chapters

At the end of each chapter, key points are highlighted followed by reflections on practice – these reflections are meant as discussion points for students and practitioners to use to help them consider and reflect on their own practice.

## Acknowledgements

Firstly, a big thank you to Keld for his unwavering support and encouragement and all the time he has spent helping me understand Danish culture.

Thank you also to all the children and pedagogues whom I have had the pleasure and privilege to work with, and to everyone at Høndruphus Nature Kindergarten, Resen Nature Kindergarten and Tumlelunden Age Integrated Day Care Centre for allowing me to use their photographs, drawings and to quote their wonderful work.

# 1 The context

This chapter looks at the geographical, social, cultural and general historical backgrounds that have shaped and influenced the use of the outdoors by the Forest School Approach in Denmark. The key features of the Danish Approach – the theory and practice; the training and roles of the pedagogues; the environment; the Danish early years curriculum; the organisation of early years settings; and the research and future of the Danish Approach – are outlined. Each of these key features is developed in more detail in subsequent chapters.

## Geography

Denmark is a small country of only 43,000 km² with approximately five and a half million inhabitants. It has an interesting geographical landscape with over 7,300 km of coastline and 407 islands; its highest point is only 170 m and apart from the four major cities of Copenhagen, Aarhus, Aalborg and Odense, two thirds of its area is rural farmland. It is the southernmost of the Nordic countries, southwest of Sweden and south of Norway, and is bordered to the south by Germany.

Historically, from the early Viking times (800–1100 AD) to the fourteenth and fifteenth centuries, Denmark's kingdom included: Norway, part of Sweden, Greenland, Iceland, the Faroe Islands and, for a time, England (King Canute 1016–1035). It now consists of Denmark and the self-governing countries of Greenland and the Faroe Islands.

## Social and cultural context

Denmark has the oldest constitutional monarchy with a multi-party parliamentary system, which means that no single political party holds an absolute majority (there are currently seven parties represented in the Danish Parliament). Danes are heavily taxed (ranging from 42 per cent to 63 per cent) but have financial security and excellent social benefits. They are proud of their democratic rights, mutual trust and freedom of speech, and they favour an informal working atmosphere and clean environment. Surveys show that Danes are the happiest in the world – based on standards of health, welfare and education (Visit Denmark 2016).

There is a generally high employment rate which means that parents need a childcare system that allows them to carry out their work. In 1976 local authorities were obliged to offer a full-time childcare place for all children between three months and school age. Most early years settings open at 6.30 a.m. and close at 5 p.m. and most schools have out-of-school centres for children before and after school times. These are usually open from 6.30 to 8 each morning and from 12 noon to 5 p.m. each afternoon (and in the school holidays these centres offer full day care).

Generally there are four types of early years care that parents can choose from:

■ Day nurseries, catering for children from 26 weeks to three years of age.

- Kindergartens, catering for children from three to six years of age.
- Age-integrated nurseries, catering for children from three months to six years.
- Childminders, catering for children from three months to three years.

The settings vary according to the geographical area they are situated in, the physical size of the setting, and the pedagogues, children and parents using the setting.

## Historical background to using the outdoors

Using the outdoors for health, leisure and education has developed from an informal part of society to an area that has both a pedagogical and political meaning. In Danish it is called *friluftsliv*, which translates as 'fresh air life', and can be seen as following three distinct phases through its history:

### Phase one

During the 1700s a change in thinking about being outdoors occurred, from one of a feeling of 'battling' with the elements for survival, to one of it being a positive aesthetic experience (Eichberg and Jespersen 2001: 28). Rousseau's thinking on nature and child upbringing also inspired people to understand the benefits of being outdoors (see Chapter Two). Literature, poems and songs were written eulogizing the beauty of nature and, especially for rich people, leisure activities such as walking and horse riding became popular.

### Phase two

By the end of the 1800s many more people were living in urban environments, an effect stemming from the industrial revolution and the need for more workers in the cities. Long working hours meant that while people had plenty of physical exercise, they had very little time to be outdoors. Many factory owners, rich landowners and trade unions arranged annual day trips for workers and their families to spend time in natural surroundings and found that these visits relieved the everyday stresses and strains of long working hours indoors. Health experts began to use the outdoors to help alleviate the illnesses brought on by an increasingly industrialised 'indoor' society. Outdoor sanatoriums and kindergartens were established so that patients and young children could have fresh air, peace in nature, and enjoy more hygienic living conditions.

Froebel's first kindergarten in Germany in 1840 inspired Danish headmaster Søren Sørensen to open a 'play and preparatory' school in 1854. He wrote: 'Children at the ages of four and five should not be imprisoned in a dirty airless schoolroom, at such a young age they should have play and movement, especially in the fresh air' (Sigsgaard 1978: 40).

In 1901 Sofus Bagger, together with his wife Hedevig, started the first *folkebørnehave* (public kindergarten for 'ordinary working people'). Bagger was very interested in school playgrounds and school gardens, and the *folkebørnehave* had hens, geese, ducks and large digging areas for the children to work and play in, as he felt these things gave city children more experiences of nature and natural things.

In 1943 John Bertelsen, one of the first trained male kindergarten pedagogues, started an adventure playground in Emdrup Banke in Copenhagen. He called this a 'junk' playground, full of old wood, tools and recycled materials for the children to construct and play with. Bertelsen laid the first foundations for 'playground pedagogy' that has been copied and developed around the world (Sigsgaard 1978: 115).

In 1952 a pedagogue named Ella Flatau started a *vandrebørnehave* (wandering kindergarten), where the children assembled at a meeting point each morning and would go off into the woods and fields for the day. At the end of the day they would assemble again at the meeting point for the parents to collect them. Later, a cabin structure was built as a meeting point and became the first nature kindergarten (Bentsen, Andkjær and Ejbye-Ernst 2009: 30).

## Phase three

The 1970s energy crisis increased people's interest in nature, firstly in the natural and political forces affecting the supply of, and demand for oil, and, secondly, a realisation of man's dependency on nature. These factors led to the recognition of the need to be more environmentally aware.

From the 1970s to the present day there has been even more focus upon nature and the environment. Through changes in patterns of work and working conditions, together with the knowledge we have about the health and educational benefits of being active outdoors, people have started using natural environments to a greater extent. Denmark takes a progressive stance on environmental preservation and rates highly in the world for 'green living'.

## The Danish Forest School Approach

The term 'Forest School' was created to describe the Danish practice of children in early years settings using the outdoors every day, all year round, as part of their pre-school education.

This practice of using the outdoors as a part of the education (and all-round child development) process is not a new phenomenon in Denmark, it has been the general practice for many years, but it is only recently that an interest has been taken in understanding the benefits to children of being and learning outdoors.

The Danish Forest School Approach came about through a number of influences, notably:

- The pedagogical theories that have influenced present-day practice.
- The training and role of pedagogues working in early years settings.
- The physical environment of settings.
- The organisation of early years settings.
- The research that has started to highlight the long-term benefits of children being outdoors.

### Theory and practice

The Danish early years pedagogical practice of using the outdoors has been influenced and supported by a number of theories and theorists from around the world including Rousseau, Pestalozzi, Froebel, Dewey, Montessori, Piaget, Vygotsky, Goleman, Gardner and Csikszentmihalyi. The theories have led to the following seven pedagogical principles of practice:

1 A holistic approach to children's learning and development.
2 Each child is unique and competent.
3 Children are active and interactive learners.
4 Children need real-life, first-hand experiences.
5 Children thrive in child-centred environments.
6 Children need time to experiment and develop independent thinking.
7 Learning comes from social interactions.

These theories and practice are elaborated in Chapter Two.

## The Danish pedagogue

The first training of pedagogues started in the early 1900s and was designed for people working with babies and young children. The present-day training has developed and now trains people to work with all age groups (cradle to grave), in a wide variety of settings. The type of training of pedagogues and the work they do is unique to Denmark; while other countries have 'pedagogues', their work is different, particularly for those working with young children. In Sweden and Norway for example, those working with children before compulsory school age are teachers and have a teacher-training background, whereas in Denmark there is a distinction between teachers and pedagogues, their training and the work they do. Pedagogy in Denmark adopts a holistic approach and works with the whole person, 'head, hands and hearts'. Childcare and education are seen as intertwined and involve learning, health, and social and emotional well-being. There is a high employment rate, with around 90 per cent of parents working outside the home, therefore a reliable and well-trained workforce is needed for pre-school age groups and for after-school care. Pedagogues are highly regarded professionals and parents view them as an essential part of their child's care and development.

A pedagogue has four main roles: firstly, to create a safe environment where children can thrive and develop in creative and stimulating surroundings; secondly, to be a role model; thirdly to support children's social and emotional development; and fourthly, to work in partnership with parents.

The training and role of Danish pedagogues is elaborated on in Chapter Three.

## The environment

The learning environment includes the indoors and outdoors. It is the interactions between the pedagogical aims, the children and adults involved, and the physical space they are in that construct the learning environment. The child's learning environment is seen holistically and includes their physical, psychological and aesthetic well-being. The learning environment is an integral part of the Danish early years curriculum, and, as part of society's democratic beliefs, children must be included in evaluating their learning environments.

Indoor environments are child-centred and uncluttered, with activities arranged on easily accessible shelves and tables. There are quiet areas with a sofa and blanket so children can snuggle up and relax. There are large cloakrooms to accommodate all the outdoor clothing for the children – each child has an area, usually with a picture of them and their name, where they can keep their clothing, footwear, etc. The cloakrooms have large drying cabinets for wet clothing and underfloor heating so that wet footwear can dry easily.

Outdoor environments have large digging areas with either sand or soil (or both) accessible, outdoor storage sheds for equipment and tools, and a large number of milk crates for the children to build with. Bikes and go-carts are usually kept to a particular area for the safety of non-bike-using children. There is a large fire pit, sometimes with a roof to keep the children dry in wet weather: during winter the fire is lit every day and usually the children and pedagogues cook on the fire at least once a week throughout the year.

Risk and challenge are a part of children's learning environments. It is seen as an important part of the Danish Approach that children learn how to assess risks and take challenges because these are vital life skills and the pedagogue's role is to support and guide the children in how to assess risks for themselves.

The learning environment is elaborated upon in Chapter Four. The chapter also discusses children's, parents, and pedagogues' attitudes to risk and challenge and what happens in the event of an accident.

## The Danish early years curriculum

The curriculum for pre-school settings in Denmark became law in 2004 and every setting has to make an institutional curriculum plan that covers six areas of learning:

- The child's all-round personal development.
- Social development.
- Language.
- Body and movement.
- Nature and natural phenomenon.
- Cultural expression and values.

The early years curriculum is described in more detail in Chapter Five, including details of recent assessments of the curriculum and subsequent changes to it.

## Organisation of settings

Inspired by the work of Froebel, Danish early years pioneers introduced a kindergarten system that included natural environments, playgrounds and opportunities for children to play outside in the fresh air, and from these the first kindergartens with a Forest School Approach emerged. This tradition of using the outdoor environment has developed into today's practice of different kinds of settings using the outdoors in their own way; a way that takes into account the people in the setting and the geographical area it is in.

Danish society's values and customs have shaped the use of the outdoors in kindergartens in their own unique and cultural way; child upbringing and the relationships between the child, the family and society are seen in a democratic and humanistic way. Parents and pedagogues place a high value on children developing their self-esteem and independence. From a very early age children are encouraged and given the opportunities to test their skills and take challenges.

Parental involvement is high in Danish kindergartens where the board of governors in each setting is mainly made up of parents, so they are actively involved in the planning, economy and day-to-day running of the setting.

Chapter Six looks at the organisation of settings in more detail, citing the organisation of three different settings: a nature kindergarten set in a forest, a nature kindergarten set by a fjord, and an age-integrated centre set in the suburbs of a town. The tools of assessment and evaluation are also discussed and examples given.

## The future of the Danish Forest School Approach

There is a growing interest in and awareness in using the outdoors for children's learning and development from parents, local politicians and schools, and this is supported by the research that has been carried out.

Many parents prefer small settings for their children, seeing them as more child-centred. This has led to an increase in the number of private forest kindergartens to meet the needs of the children and their families.

Some local politicians see forest kindergartens as being healthier for children and pedagogues and they see the building of more forest kindergartens as an investment in children's futures.

Underpinning the Danish Forest School Approach is research that indicates that using the outdoor environment and allowing children to be outdoors all year round is beneficial. It not only develops children's physical, cognitive, linguistic, social and emotional competencies, it also keeps them healthy. The research shows that children who spend a significant length of time outdoors each day have better social skills, are more attentive, have fewer infections, have fewer conflicts, have better brain function, have better language development and learn vital life skills.

The early years practice of using the outdoors as a learning environment, together with the research that indicates that being outdoors is motivational for learning, means that Danish schools have started to introduce 'outdoor schooling'.

This interest in the Approach appears to suggest that in future there will be more forest and nature kindergartens and school children will have more opportunities for learning outside the classroom.

Chapter Seven looks at the future of Forest Schools in Denmark.

## Key points

1  The context of using the outdoors for health, leisure and education has developed from an informal part of society to an area that has both a pedagogical and political meaning.
2  The use of the outdoors helps to alleviate illnesses that are brought on by a more urban and industrialised society.
3  A realisation of man's dependency on nature for food and energy has led to a recognition of the need to be more environmentally aware.
4  The historical, social, political and cultural context is a major factor in the development of the Danish Forest School Approach.
5  The early nature kindergartens were built upon the belief that young children needed play and fresh air in order to develop and that, especially for city children, they should have more experiences of nature and natural things.
6  The Danish Forest School Approach has come about through a number of influences – the theory and practice; the training and roles of the pedagogues; the environment; and the organisation of early years settings.
7  The Danish Approach takes a holistic view of children's learning and development and views each child as unique and competent.
8  Children are seen as active and interactive learners needing real-life and first-hand experiences, and time to experiment and develop independent thinking.

9   Children thrive in child-centred environments and learning comes from social interactions.
10  Child upbringing and relationships between the child, the family and society are seen in a democratic and humanistic way.

## Reflections on the Danish Forest School Approach

1   Background and context:
   ■ Do you know the contextual background to your practice?
   ■ What has influenced your practice most?
   ■ Do you and your colleagues discuss practice and share experiences?

2   Using the outdoors:
   ■ How do you view your setting's outdoor environment?
   ■ If structurally possible, do you allow for free-flow so that the children have free access to the outdoors?
   ■ Do you and your colleagues have a collective belief about using the outdoors and value these experiences?

3   Values:
   ■ What are the principle values that you think children should develop and learn in early years settings?
   ■ Are these values shared by the practitioners, children and parents?

4   Relationships with parents:
   ■ Do you encourage parents to be actively involved in the function and daily practices within your setting?
   ■ In what ways can parents be more involved?
   ■ Are parents involved in outdoor activities?
   ■ Do the parents know and understand your reasons for using the outdoor environment every day and all year round?

5   Policies and documents:
   ■ Do your policies, documents and website clearly state your pedagogy and philosophy for using the outdoor environment?
   ■ Can you write a few sentences to communicate your enthusiasm and imagination in using the outdoors in your setting?

# References

Bentsen, P., Andkjær, S. and Ejbye-Ernst, N. (2009) *Frilusftliv. Natur, Samfund og Pædagogik.* [Friluftliv. Nature, Society and Pedagogy]. Copenhagen: Munksgaard.

Eichberg, H. and Jespersen, E. (2001) *De Grønne Bølger. Træk af Natur – og Friluftslivets Historier.* [The Green Waves. Episodes of Nature and Friluftsliv History]. In Bentsen, P., Andkjær, S. and Ejbye-Ernst, N. (2009) *Frilusftliv. Natur, Samfund og Pædagogik.* [Friluftliv. Nature, Society and Pedagogy]. Copenhagen: Munksgaard.

Sigsgaard, J. (1978) *Folkebørnehave og Socialpædagogik.* [The People's Kindergarten and Social Pedagogy]. Copenhagen: Børne og Unge.

Visit Denmark. (2016) *Happiest people in the world.* www.visitdenmark.co.uk/en-gb/denmark/art/happiest-people-world. Accessed 11 April 2016

# 2 | Theory and practice

This chapter looks at the Danish early years pedagogical practice of using the outdoors that has been influenced and supported by a number of theories and theorists from around the world including Rousseau, Pestalozzi, Froebel, Dewey, Montessori, Piaget, Vygotsky, Goleman, Gardner and Csikszentmihalyi. The theories have led to the following seven pedagogical principles of practice:

1   A holistic approach to children's learning and development.
2   Each child is unique and competent.

3   Children are active and interactive learners.
4   Children need real-life, first-hand experiences.
5   Children thrive in child-centred environments.
6   Children need time to experiment and develop independent thinking.
7   Learning comes from social interactions.

Each principle is expanded upon and the theories supporting the principle explained, followed by an example of present-day practice supporting the theories.

## A holistic approach to children's learning and development

A holistic approach to learning is concerned with the development of every child's intellectual, emotional, social, physical, creative and spiritual potential; it seeks to engage children in the learning process and encourages personal and collective responsibility. Key factors involved with a holistic approach are that children understand:

- *Themselves* – to have self-respect and self-esteem.
- *Relationships with others* – adults and other children.
- *Resilience* – overcoming difficulties and taking challenges.
- *Aesthetics* – the beauty of their natural surroundings and having awe and wonder in life.

### Supporting theories

Jean-Jacques Rousseau, in his work *Emile*, published in 1762, described a pedagogical way of thinking that took its starting point in a child's reality and natural surroundings, believing that from children's experiences of the natural, real world around them they construct their understanding and knowledge. Rousseau said that we expect to train a young child by making him reason, but this is starting at the end of the process and that if children understood how to reason they wouldn't need to be educated! In his book a boy called Emile is to be raised in the countryside – which Rousseau believed to be a more healthy and natural environment than the city – together with a pedagogue tutor who would guide him through various learning experiences (Wu 1979).

Johann Heinrich Pestalozzi took Rousseau's ideas and developed them into a workable, child-centred pedagogy. In his book *How Gertrude Teaches Her Children*, published in 1801, he illuminated the ideas of pedagogy through actual practice; he believed that children learn through activity and doing things. He emphasised that every aspect of the child's life contributed to the formation of personality, character and reason (Channing 2009).

## Present-day practice

In a nature kindergarten set in woodland the pedagogues take the children out each day for a walk around 'their' forest. As they walk they talk about changes they can see – man- and animal-made (tracks, chewed pine cones, nests, etc.) and seasonal changes (leaves, temperature, etc.). Some things they investigate *in situ* using the tools they have brought with them, some things they take back to the kindergarten for further investigation and research. The pedagogues listen to the children and prompt and support their interest in what they see and find. By going out each day in the same environment all year round, the children construct their understanding and knowledge of their world; and together with the pedagogues they try to understand why things are the way they are and to begin to understand their place in nature. This kindergarten, like many others, has a 'wonder cabinet' made of glass in which children can put the things that they have brought back from the forest. They can return to these over and over again, reliving the time they were found, comparing them with similar new finds, discussing with peers and the pedagogues the possibilities around how the artefacts came to be. For example, there's a snake skin: this was a special find and one that intrigues the children; they ask many questions, such as, 'how can the snake live without its skin?', which leads the children and pedagogues to get out their reference books and spend time discussing what they learn.

## Each child is unique and competent

Every child is unique and competent in their own way, and the way they think, feel and interact with others reflects their uniqueness and competence. Some children are outgoing and some are shy, some show a preference for physical activities and some children love stories and music.

To view the child as unique and competent is to see his or her potential. Children need an environment in which they can flourish and grow and develop positive self-esteem.

## Supporting theories

Howard Gardner's multiple intelligence theory (MI) asserts that all people possess a set of intelligences, not just one type and level of intelligence. Historically, intelligence was thought to be measurable on a single scale; as Gardner states:

> Intelligence is a term for organising and describing human capabilities, rather than a reference to some commodity inside the head. An intelligence is not a 'thing', but rather a potential, the presence of which allows an individual access to forms of thinking appropriate to specific kinds of content.
>
> (Gardner 1993: 59)

One of Gardner's intelligences is 'Naturalist Intelligence', which enables us to recognise, categorise and draw upon certain features of the environment. Some children, from an early age, are good at recognising and classifying artefacts. Children with a preference for Naturalist Intelligence enjoy playing with pets, investigating nature and raising animals and need opportunities for interacting with animals and using real tools for investigating nature.

We need to note that Gardner's MI theory should not be used to pigeonhole children – children are a mixture of learning styles and preferences and not just a single type. The types of intelligences that a person possesses indicate not only a person's capability, but also the manner or method in which they prefer to learn and develop their strengths and their weaknesses.

Mihaly Csikszentmihalyi's theory of flow supports Danish pedagogical practices, as its roots are firmly based in creativity and the development of human potential. At its simplest, the theory is that people are most happy when completely absorbed in an activity they are engaged in, and that we learn and remember most when we are happy. Happiness in Csikszentmihalyi's theory means being totally involved in an activity and using one's skills to the utmost (Csikszentmihalyi 2002).

Figure 2.1 illustrates the theory of flow, or optimal, learning:

- If a child is asked to perform a low challenge and has low capabilities, they have apathy.

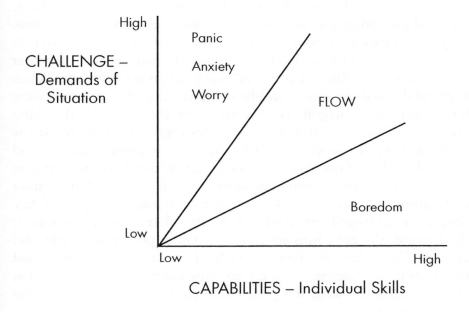

**Figure 2.1 Flow, or optimal, learning (capabilities and challenges)**

■ If a child is asked to perform a low challenge and has high capabilities, they are bored.
■ If a child is asked to perform a high challenge and they have low capabilities, they panic and are anxious.
■ If a child is asked to perform a challenge that is equal or slightly higher than their capabilities, they are in flow.

Offering children uninteresting, unstimulating experiences does not physically or intellectually challenge them, and this usually leads to disruptive behaviour. But if the context includes a reasonable amount of complexity and challenge, children are more likely to take the initiative, respond to the challenge and acquire important skills and concepts.

## Present-day practice

When Kristian first started at the nature kindergarten he was shy and did not mix with the other children. He stayed close to the pedagogue when they went out for their daily walk through the forest. On these daily walks the children love to discover things in the environment – insects, plants, trees – and the pedagogue takes time to answer the children's questions. The pedagogue explains to the children why certain plants and animals live in the forest, and why it is that for some animals we just find their tracks but never see them. It appeared that Kristian was interested, even though he did not say much, and he enjoyed using the tools that were taken out each day – magnifiers, collecting pots, etc. and he liked looking at the books about nature back in the kindergarten. Throughout the autumn and winter he continued to show his interest in nature and started asking lots of questions. The pedagogues could see that Kristian was very keen to have nature experiences and spent a lot of time either investigating outdoors or looking at nature books indoors. His key pedagogue encouraged him to tell her and the other children about what he had found; she gave him an exercise book to put photographs and drawings of his nature discoveries into. By the next summer term he had become one of the 'leaders' of the group, showing younger children what he had found and asking the pedagogue deeper questions about the plants and animals.

## Children are active and interactive learners

The active engagement of children in the learning process and their engagement with others in interactive activities, or engagement with materials, forms the dynamics for knowledge and understanding. Through active learning, children are constantly changing, adjusting and rearranging meaning and their understanding of things. Children are interested in experiments, trial and error, and representing what they are learning through construction and play. Active learning takes place with experiences, for example children will learn more about the seasons in nature by being outdoors at different times of the year and actually experiencing the changes in the weather, rather than hearing a story about the seasons.

### Supporting theories

John Dewey believed that children learn by doing and that in the outdoor environment children are active and interactive participants in their learning processes. He felt that children must be engaged in an active quest for learning and new ideas. Dewey thought that children learn best when they interact with other people, working both alone and cooperatively with peers and adults. According to Dewey, children's interests form the basis for curriculum planning, believing that the interests and background of each child and group must be considered when educators plan learning experiences (Mooney 2000: 5).

Dewey thought that rather than saying 'the children will enjoy this', teachers need to ask the following questions when they plan activities:

- How does this expand on what these children already know?
- How will this activity help these children to grow?
- What skills are being developed?
- How will this activity help these children come to know more about their world?
- How does this activity prepare these children to live more fully?

Dewey believed that education is part of life and should involve real-life experiences and that teachers should encourage experimentation and independent thinking.

At the time of Jean Piaget's investigations into children's learning in the early 1900s it was generally believed that learning was either intrinsic (coming from the child) or extrinsic (imposed by the environment or adults); Piaget felt that neither position explained learning by itself, rather it was the child's interactions with his environment and with adults that create learning. Piaget believed that children construct their own knowledge by giving meaning to the people, places and things in their world. He believed that teachers should:

- Provide large blocks of free play time – when children are interested and involved their absorption needs to be respected and they should be given the time to complete their play and should have the opportunity to 'save' their play to return to later and build on it if they wish.
- Provide real world experiences – children learn best from first-hand real-life experiences; Piaget believed this is what construction of knowledge is all about for young children.
- Plan open-ended activities and ask open-ended questions as these support children's cognitive development because they require children to think for themselves and puts them in the position of being an inquirer, rather than in the position of being right or wrong.

(Mooney 2000: 74–76)

## Present-day practice

In a nature kindergarten that is set in an old farm, the children and peda-gogues made a vegetable garden where they planted potatoes, leeks, beetroots, onions and carrots. At harvest time everyone was busy picking the vegetables; there were too many for them to eat, so they put the surplus by the entry door and the pedagogues helped the children to make a 'For Sale' sign so that when the parents came to collect their children they could buy the fresh vegetables. The children were excited to put more vegetables out for sale each day and enjoyed collecting the money for them. The whole process of planting, picking and selling turned into a term-long project. All areas of the curriculum were covered in a meaningful, first-hand way and all the children and pedagogues worked side-by-side. The parents said how much the children enjoyed helping them to prepare and eat the vegetables at home – one parent said that when he was at the supermarket with his child, she said to another shopper by the vegetable counter, 'You know you can grow these in your garden. It's easy but if you don't want to you can come and buy some of ours at the kindergarten'!

## Children need real-life, first-hand experiences

Children are by nature observers and explorers and through real-life, first-hand experiences they develop an understanding of themselves and the environment they are in.

Children learn by doing everyday tasks in real-life situations, using real tools and materials. A child's all-round physical, emotional, social, linguistic, cognitive and sensory development is fostered through actual first-hand experiences.

## Supporting theories

Maria Montessori suggested that the size of furnishings and materials was important. When she opened her kindergartens in Italy at the beginning of the twentieth century, child-sized tools and furnishings were not available, so she began to make her own. Montessori believed that children needed real tools and materials if they were to do the work that interested them – sharp knives, good scissors, woodworking and cleaning tools. She was also aware of the importance of children's sensory development and believed that children learn through sensory experiences with textures, sights and smells (Mooney 2000: 24).

Jean Piaget also believed that it is important for children to experience whatever we want them to learn about. He believed that by giving children real-world experiences we are enabling them to construct knowledge (Mooney 2000: 62).

## Present-day practice

Last summer, while out on their daily walk, a group of children and their pedagogue came across a forester who was cutting the thin lower branches off some fir trees. They watched him and asked lots of questions. The pedagogue asked if they could take some of the branches back to their kindergarten for the goats to eat; they all carried as many branches as they could manage and returned to the kindergarten for lunch. During lunchtime two of the children, Amelia and Jakob, talked about the fir tree branches and the work of the forester. After lunch the pedagogue went outside with her group and they started to put the fir branches in the goat pen. Amelia and Jakob asked if they could keep some of the branches as they wanted to make something with them. The pedagogue agreed and gave them permission to go into the tool store to get hammers and nails (the tools they said they needed). For the next two hours they worked hard with the branches and by three in the afternoon stood back in satisfaction – they had made a fir tree! The pedagogue asked them what they had done, and why, and they explained that they thought it was sad to see the branches cut off, so they had decided to 'put the tree back together again'. The following day they returned to their 'fir tree' and planted it in the middle of the large sand pit; they then started collecting things to hang on its branches – small plastic sand toys, pieces of rope. The two children then called over their friends and said, 'It's Christmas, let's dance around the tree!'

## Children thrive in child-centred environments

The starting point of child-centred environments is the concept of children using the spaces; all children's needs must be taken into account. The way that materials are placed at child height, the use of child-sized furnishings and the layout of the area in a way that is aesthetically pleasing and welcoming: all indicate that the adults have carefully considered the children's world. There should be space for children's personal belongings, large enough cloakrooms and child-sized toilets with mirrors and washbasins at their height. A child-centred environment takes into account the rhythms of young children's daily lives, including the need for restful areas, places for children who need a sleep time and creative areas. There should be interconnectedness between indoors and outdoors and an understanding that children need to feel in harmony with the environment.

## Supporting theories

Froebel believed that the period of childhood is a special time when children develop their character and knowledge, and that the education of young children should therefore be child-centred to match their developmental characteristics. For Froebel, the kindergarten was a garden for children to flourish and grow in (Sigsgaard 1978: 36).

Montessori believed that child-centred environments not only included the space children use and the furnishings and materials within that space, but also the adults and the children who share their days with each other. Montessori believed that children learn without conscious effort from the environments where they spend their time. Montessori also developed child-sized materials and equipment so that children could accomplish their tasks and be safe and comfortable (Mooney 2000: 24).

## Present-day practice

In an integrated-age day-care setting, eleven of the six-month to three-year-olds are having lunch together with their three pedagogues. The pedagogues place plates of cold meats, bowls of cut-up vegetables, butter and baskets of sliced bread on the table. Plates, knives and forks, glasses and small glass jugs are also placed on the table. The children take a slice of bread and butter it (some with help from a pedagogue), they choose a slice of meat and some vegetables and start eating. One of the pedagogues asks each child if they would like milk or water to drink and then pours the drink into a small glass jug. The child then takes the small jug and pours into their glass. The pedagogical thinking behind this is that the child is independent and competent and the pedagogues support this development by the children selecting their own food and pouring their own drink (the glass jug is child sized and if the child does spill any it is only a small amount that can be easily mopped up). After lunch the children start to get ready for sleep time; in the bathroom each child has a basket with their own clothes in, this basket is placed on the floor by the side of the child and they change their clothes with help from the pedagogue. The children then go outside to their large wooden pram for a sleep. There's a wooden ladder for each child to climb up into their pram and they have a harness to keep them safely in the pram and a special toy or comforter from home to cuddle up with. Outside sleep time is used all year round – summer and winter, up to –20°C, as this is seen to be the healthiest for young children.

## Children need time to experiment and develop independent thinking

Children need time to play, to explore and to experiment with their ideas and knowledge. They need time to try things out, make mistakes, try something else, repeat their play and consolidate their ideas. Children should have the possibility, if feasible, to 'save' their constructions and materials, so they can return to them the next day.

Providing large blocks of open-ended playtime offers children the opportunity to combine their ideas, impressions and intuitions, with experiences and opinions. They create ideas about their world and share them with one another. They establish a culture and a social world with their peers. This kind of play allows children the time to make sense of their experiences and discover the joy of fellowship. When it is self-directed, play leads to feelings of competence and self-confidence.

## Supporting theories

Montessori believed that children have the capacity for great concentration when they have interesting things to do and are given the freedom and time to do them (Mooney 2000: 30).

Piaget believed that children should have large blocks of free play time because when they are interested and involved their absorption needs to be respected and they should be given the time to complete their play and have the opportunity to return to it later and build upon it if they wish (Mooney 2000: 74).

Csikszentmihalyi believes that when a child is in flow – that is when the challenge of an activity or task is equal or slightly higher than their capabilities, they become absorbed in what they are doing. When a child is in flow they concentrate for long periods and this is the time of optimal learning. Therefore, to enable children to be in the flow zone, practitioners need to give children time (Csikszentmihalyi 2002).

## Present-day practice

A collection of tools for investigating nature is generally available in all kindergartens, but in a nature kindergarten the tools are an essential ingredient of everyday life. Many nature kindergartens have at least one pull-along trolley full of hand lenses, bug containers, reference materials, knives and saws that can be taken out on a walk through nature. The children learn how to use the tools safely and responsibly and enjoy being able to select for themselves the tool they want to use to investigate the varied plant and animal life around them. In one nature kindergarten, the children decided that they wanted to build a shelter so they would have a base to be able to spend time in a particular area that fascinated them. Back at the kindergarten the pedagogue asked them what tools they thought they would need to make the base. The children decided that they needed something to help them cut branches and this enabled the pedagogue to introduce them to secateurs and loppers, which she showed them how to use. The next day the tools were added to the trolley and taken to the base site and over the next few days the children and pedagogue made a base. That was two years ago: since then the base has been mended and added to and has also been replicated in other parts of the forest.

## Learning comes from social interactions

Through daily interactions with responsive, affectionate adults, young children experience positive social relationships. Self-confidence develops and children learn to communicate their needs and master challenges in their world. Young children thrive when they encounter challenges they can meet; they flourish when they are free to explore and feel that caring adults encourage and take pleasure in their emerging interests and skills.

## Supporting theories

Lev Vygotsky showed that social and cognitive development work together and build on each other; he believed that learning takes place in the social world when children and adults play and learn together.

One of the most important concepts of Vygotsky's theory is that of the Zone of Proximal Development (ZPD) which he believed was the distance between the most difficult task a child can do alone and the most difficult task a child can do with help – either from an adult or another child. This help from an adult or child he called scaffolding; just as builders use scaffolding to enable them to climb higher and to keep them safe while constructing a building. Vygotsky's theoretical framework is based upon his belief that social interaction plays a fundamental role in the development of cognition.

Vygotsky states, 'every function in the child's cultural development appears twice: first, on the social level, and later, on the individual level; first between people (inter-psychological) and then inside the child (intra-psychological)' (Vygotsky 1978: 57).

Daniel Goleman's work explores a theory of human social intelligence, and believes that man is designed for sociability, constantly engaged in what he calls a 'neural ballet' that connects us brain-to-brain with those around us. Goleman believes that through social play young children find a secure space to try out new things and experiences with minimum anxiety. Social, playful activity produces great feelings of pleasure, which in turn release vital hormones in our brains that promote all-round development. He says:

> A simple sign that a child feels he has a safe haven is going out to play. Playful fun has serious benefits; through years of hard play, children acquire a range of social expertise. For one, they learn social savvy, like how to negotiate power struggles, how to cooperate and form alliances, and how to concede with grace.
>
> (Goleman 2006: 178)

## Present-day practice

A group of boys are playing in the large sand area: two boys are digging in the sand and after a time start to make a tunnel from one hole to the other. In another part of the sand area two other boys are making roads for the cars they have brought outside. Each pair of boys plays their games for a time, then seem to become aware of one another for the first time: 'Hey, that's a great tunnel you've made, can we build a road to the tunnel and drive our cars through?' So starts a cooperative project between the boys – more tunnels are made and more cars brought out. The boys spend the two-hour period before lunch immersed in their play, and as soon as lunch is over they run back to continue playing in the sand area. From snatches of overheard conversation between them one can hear them problem solving and inventing; from the way they talk and the looks of eager concentration it appears that they are happy.

## Key points

1   Significant pedagogical theories have influenced present-day practice.
2   A holistic approach to learning promotes children's all-round development.
3   Each child is unique and competent and needs an environment that encourages the development of their self-esteem.
4   Children need challenges that are in keeping with their skills to maintain their motivation and interest.
5   Children are active and interactive learners and through active learning experiences they form their understanding and knowledge.
6   Practitioners need to be reflective when planning activities.
7   Children need real-life first-hand experiences to enable them to develop an understanding of themselves and the environment they are in.
8   Children thrive in child-centred environments and practitioners need to place the child at the centre of their planning of early years environments.
9   Children need time to experiment and develop independent thinking so that they can consolidate their ideas and learning.
10  Learning comes from social interactions with peers and adults.

## Reflections on practice

1   Experiences in nature:
    ■ Do you set up areas and provide a variety of materials that provide rich learning experiences?

- How do you encourage children to become engaged in activities that are multi-sensory and engage all parts of the brain?
- How can you extend outdoor activities to the indoors by bringing nature inside to build on children's learning experiences?
- How could you be more personally aware in nature to help children notice and discuss seasonal changes, habitats, living creatures, etc.?

2  First-hand experiences:
- Do you engage children in real work that has a purpose?
- How do you monitor safety and conflict and show children how to use materials, tools and their bodies safely?
- In what ways do you allow appropriate risk taking?
- How can you allow children to explore materials and tools in their own way and use their imaginations to change the function of materials?

3  Adult-child relationships:
- Do you listen carefully to children when they talk about their plans and discoveries, and how do you extend their interest?
- What strategies do you use to allow children to problem-solve and learn without intervening too early?
- In which ways do you collaborate with children?

4  Open-ended time and questions:
- What questions do you ask children to encourage them to think, problem-solve and put what they know into words?
- How can you help children interact successfully with other children?
- Does your planning allow flexibility so you can extend activities to allow more time for children to deepen their experiences?

5  Scaffolding and building on children's strengths:
- How do you invite children to draw, sketch and document their observations, their memories, and to help them internalise their experiences?
- In what ways can you provide specific learning experiences that connect to children's prior knowledge?
- Do you accommodate each child's needs and interests and build on them?

# References

Channing, E. (2009) *Pestalozzi's Leonard and Gertrude.* London: BiblioBazaar.

Csikszentmihalyi, M. (2002) *Flow: The Psychology of Happiness: The Classic Work on How to Achieve Happiness.* London: Random House.

Gardner, H. (1993) *Frames of Mind.* New York: Basic Books.

Goleman, D. (2006) *Social Intelligence. The New Science of Human Relationships.* New York: Hutchinson.

Mooney, C.G. (2000) *Theories of Childhood: An Introduction to Dewey, Montessori, Erickson, Piaget and Vygotsky.* Minnesota: Redleaf Press.

Sigsgaard, J. (1978) *Folkebørnehave og Socialpædagogik.* [The People's Kindergarten and Social Pedagogy]. Copenhagen: Børne og Unge.

Vygotsky, L. (1978) *Mind in Society.* Cambridge MA: Harvard University Press.

Wu, M. (1979) *Emile. J.J. Rousseau.* New York: Basic Books.

# 3 | The Danish pedagogue

This chapter looks at the history, training and role of pedagogues in Denmark from the first one-year training at the beginning of the 1900s to the present-day three-and-a-half-year bachelor-level education. Today pedagogues are trained to work in a variety of settings with people of all ages – children, young people and adults, and to take a holistic approach to learning, development and care. The chapter then goes on to look at the four main roles that a pedagogue has in Danish early years settings: first to create a safe environment where children can thrive and develop in a creatively stimulating surrounding; second to be a role model; third to support children's social and emotional development; and fourth to work in partnership with parents.

## What does 'pedagogue' mean?

In order to understand the work of pedagogues in Denmark one first needs to understand the terms pedagogue and pedagogy in their Danish contexts.

The word pedagogue comes from the Greek *paidagogeo,* which means 'to lead the child'. In ancient Greece the *paidagogos* was a slave who took his master's son (girls were not publicly taught) to school and supervised his instruction (Williams-Siegfredsen 2007: 66).

Danish pedagogy (and the training of pedagogues) stems from the theories outlined in Chapter Two and from Danish culture and history (political, social and societal). Pedagogical work cannot be defined as carrying out particular actions or methods; it involves the establishment of different types of social life, educations and environments, based on and supported by specific norms and values. As a discipline pedagogy is closely linked to philosophy. The ideal is a free and competent individual. Values and opportunities are discussed in relation to this ideal and connected to issues relating to man's individual needs and requirements (psychology and biology) and to questions of social conditions and opportunities (sociology).

Pedagogical work adopts a holistic approach to children, young people and adults, starting from the whole person, and includes body, mind, emotions, creativity and social identity. This has been referred to by many as 'head, hands and hearts'. It transcends the division between 'childcare' and 'education', as pedagogy regards care as inseparably linked with learning, health, and social and emotional well-being.

Pedagogues are highly regarded professionals in Denmark. Parents and society as a whole see them as an essential part of the care, welfare and education sector, and, as they are trained to work in a multi-disciplinary way, they work in a variety of settings covering education, social welfare, health and criminal services, with all age groups of people. In Denmark over 97 per cent of children aged three to five are in some form of day-care facility and parent satisfaction surveys show that parents are very happy with the day-care provision their children have (*Børne og Unge* 2014).

## The training of pedagogues in Denmark

The first training of pedagogues grew from Froebel's thoughts on children's upbringing and kindergartens, and in 1880 Sophus and Hedevig Bagger began training 'kindergarten school mistresses' as they were then called. The Froebel Training College started in 1904, offering one-year training and in 1918 the training became a two-year course. In 1928 Sofie Rifbjerg started a training course based on Montessori's theories. This college was known as the Seminariet for Småbørnepædagoger (Training College for Small Children's Pedagogues).

During the 1930s there were also political and social developments that affected pedagogy and kindergartens, in particular a huge house rebuilding scheme to give better health and social conditions to children and families. New houses were built out of the large cities, giving children and their families green spaces and a healthier lifestyle in more natural surroundings. Despite Denmark being occupied by Germany in 1940, the number of day-care institutions grew and new initiatives started, such as John Bertelsen's adventure playground in Emdrup Banke (Sigsgaard 1978: 114).

During the 1950s and 1960s more women came into the workforce, partly because there was a need for a larger workforce and partly because of movements such as 'women's liberation'. This led to a huge increase in childcare settings, which meant the need for more pedagogues. In 1970 the pedagogue training period was increased from two to three years and many more training colleges emerged throughout Denmark. At that time there were three separate training routes for those working in:

- Kindergartens and day nurseries.
- Recreation centres, out-of-school centres and 24-hour service institutions.
- Institutions for children, young people and adults with reduced psychological or physical capacities, adults with social problems, family institutions and child and youth psychiatric hospitals.

For each kind of training, the three-year education was very practical and practice-based, with over one third of the time spent out in practice placements and the remaining college-taught part split between theoretical subjects (pedagogy, psychology and social sciences) and what were called culture and activity subjects (art, drama, music, nature study and Danish).

In November 1990 a new Education Act was passed by Parliament to integrate the three types of training into one general three-and-a-half year education to provide:

> a generalist education, with the purpose of educating pedagogues that can solve pedagogical tasks, regardless of if the tasks concern children, young people or adults, that have social problems, psychological or physical handicaps, or concern children, young people and adults that have no such problems.
>
> (Bayer *et al.* 1994: 36)

The new training programme also contained two extra theoretical subjects, sociology and anthropology, with the aim of giving new perspectives on childhood and children's learning.

In the 1990s, international developments had effects on the training and work of pedagogues, such as the pedagogy of Reggio Emilia, which inspired many Danish early years settings to change their traditional group rooms into differentiated function rooms for art, adventure, reading, etc. The documentation of children's play, life and activities was introduced in nearly all settings. Also during this time a 'care guarantee' was introduced by Parliament, guaranteeing parents a full-time childcare place for children from six months of age.

In 2001 a new qualification of professional bachelor for pedagogues (also for teachers, nurses and physiotherapists) came into being. The numerous small training colleges for each type of education were amalgamated into larger, polytechnic-type institutions, known as 'CVUs' (Centres of Higher Education).

An evaluation of the generalised pedagogue training was presented in spring 2003 and it was critical of the training, which it saw as too general (cradle to grave for all user groups) and lacking a professional core. This evaluation led to two major changes, the first being an even more centralised professional higher education system, whereby the centres of higher education amalgamated into eight university colleges. Second, the pedagogue training was changed in 2007 to include a generalist first part and a specialised second part. Pedagogue students now choose to specialise in one of the following three areas:

- Children and young people.
- People with special needs.
- People with social difficulties.

The 2007 programme of training was changed in 2014. The biggest change in the training is a focus on 'competence goals', which are listed for each subject and specialisation area. The first year of training is common for all students and forms a foundation in pedagogy. In the second year, the students choose one of three specialised areas:

1 Childcare pedagogy (0–5 years).
2 School and out-of-school pedagogy (6–18 years).
3 Social and special pedagogy (all ages).

The training is modularised, each module lasting six to seven weeks. There are seven obligatory modules and two that the students can choose from:

- Creative expressions.
- Nature and outdoor life.
- Health promotion and exercise.
- Media and digital culture.
- Culture projects and cultural organisation
- Social innovation and entrepreneurship creation.
- Culture encounters and interculturalism.

There are now four practice periods – two lasting six months and two shorter ones, the fourth and final period being connected to students' bachelor project and the specialised area they have chosen in connection with it.

The political intention in changing pedagogue training is to bring the training closer to practice, to strengthen interdisciplinary work and to provide more flexibility in the training (*Børne og Unge* 2014).

## The role of the pedagogue in early years settings

The role of the pedagogue, be it in a specific forest or nature kindergarten or in any other early years setting, starts by adopting a holistic approach to the child, which includes the body, mind, emotions, creativity and social identity.

Danish law stipulates that pedagogues in early years settings must:

- Promote children's well-being, health, development and learning.

- Support the individual child's all-round development and self-esteem.
- Promote children's learning and the development of competencies.
- Give children a voice, responsibility and an understanding of democracy.
- Develop children's independence and their ability to enter into a responsible community.

In order to achieve these demands there are four main roles that a pedagogue must fulfil:

1  Create a safe environment where children can thrive and develop in creatively stimulating surroundings.
2  Be a role model.
3  Support children's social and emotional development.
4  Work in partnership together with parents.

## Create a safe environment where children can thrive and develop in creatively stimulating surroundings

The pedagogue's role is to set the framework and possibilities for children to experience activities and materials, and give them space and time to develop their experiences and understanding. Through careful observations, pedagogues can introduce children to new materials that they feel will motivate them to deepen their understanding and learning. The pedagogue's role is one of co-constructor, coach and facilitator, and they need to be sensitive as to when they step into an activity or game, and when to step back from it and allow the children time on their own. Children need the possibilities of initiating their own play and using materials creatively and imaginatively. For example: milk crates can become a train or a boat or a castle; a tree can be a climbing frame or a desert island or a home under its canopy of leaves. Children need an environment that motivates them to investigate and develop their emotional, social, intellectual, linguistic and sensory skills.

The pedagogues provide an indoor environment that is comfortable and homely where children can have areas to relax in and areas for more active pursuits. It should be an uncluttered and attractive place to be. The Danish word *hygge* means a cosy, comfortable, warm feeling; the pedagogues use this word when they describe how they welcome the children and parents each day. Particularly on cold dark winter mornings it is important to feel that you are entering a cosy, comfortable, warm place. The pedagogues light candles at the entrance and inside the kindergarten; they bake bread each morning, so that when the children arrive there is the lovely smell of freshly baked bread. The environment also needs to be homely because many children spend a lot of hours in childcare settings: up to eight hours a day, for up to 47 weeks a year is fairly average.

The pedagogues provide an outdoor environment that is motivating for children to be in: tools and equipment are easily accessible; there are areas for digging, bike riding, water play, and quiet areas for sitting. Most nature and forest kindergartens have animals – hens, goats, horses, pigs, rabbits – and the pedagogues and children look after them together. The children are involved in the feeding, watering and cleaning of the animals and they learn to take responsibility in the care of living creatures through their first-hand experiences.

Using the natural resources around them, the pedagogues help children to learn life skills. Taking children out into the water of the fjord, the pedagogue explains why they need waders and life vests. The children love going out into the water, it is exciting and gives different sensations to the body.

**Figure 3.1 Pedagogue and child, fishing**

## Be a role model

The pedagogue shows by their own example how to behave. They do this by showing respect to the children, colleagues and parents, demonstrating how to speak to one another, showing how others can be affected by our actions, modelling the importance of listening to people and demonstrating how to make people visiting the kindergarten welcome. The pedagogue also needs to be a role model of democracy – turn taking, giving 'space' when needed, and valuing people for themselves.

The pedagogues need to show that they are motivated and engaged when outdoors, in all weathers, every day, all year round. They need to be engaged, inquisitive and imaginative and support the same attributes in the children. They need to be knowledgeable and able to show children how to find things out for themselves. By eating together with the children they model social manners – passing food and drink to one another, asking for something, chatting about everyday things, saying 'please' and 'thank you'.

Sune and Henrik are two pedagogues working at Tumlelunden age-integrated childcare centre. When discussing the pedagogue as a role model for children, they say:

> From our point of view, a good role model is a pedagogue that really desires to show the way for children, but also one that really desires to be in the background and believes in the child's own ability. A pedagogue must be true and alive in their role, have engagement, interest and courage to investigate something new and generally have fun within the pedagogical field and let their own inner child come out.
>
> (Extract from email sent 6 July 2016)

## Support children's social and emotional development

With the surroundings and the materials they provide, pedagogues support children as they begin to regulate their emotions and develop a sense of predictability, safety and responsiveness in their social environments. Pedagogues talk to children about feelings and acknowledge them by, for example, putting words to them, saying things like, 'I can see that you're feeling angry.' In this way the pedagogues encourage children to understand their feelings and begin to find ways of dealing with their emotions. Social and emotional well-being includes intra- and interpersonal processes. The way we identify and understand our feelings, the

**Figure 3.2 Role-playing**

feelings of others and relationships, are at an emerging stage in young children's development and are supported by the pedagogues through their holistic work with them.

As mentioned earlier, most nature and forest kindergartens keep animals and the pedagogues believe this promotes children's social and emotional development. The children are naturally fascinated by the animals and gain much pleasure from touching them. From working alongside the pedagogues the children learn caring skills and they learn about the processes of life. The pedagogues talk a lot about the animals to the children and about the need to look after them properly. Occasionally an animal becomes ill or dies and the pedagogue sensitively talks about this with the children, using the event as an important learning opportunity to talk about life and death and life-cycle processes. Pedagogues understand that emotion and cognition work together and that by giving children emotional well-being they are also promoting children's learning.

It was nearly lunchtime and the children were hungry: they had had a long walk out in the forest, and it was time to go back to the kindergarten. Suddenly, the children found some bones beneath a tree and all thoughts of lunch disappeared! The children searched around the area and found more bones and brought them to the pedagogue. They talked about what kind of animal the bones were from and the pedagogue pointed out different features of the bones; judging by the skull it was a bird, quite a big one. The children named all the large birds they could think of and the pedagogue talked about the other bones: 'This one's a thigh bone, look at its shape. You have bones like this too, feel your thigh – can you feel the bone inside? It has a larger bit at the top, can you feel it?' Nikoli was thrilled: 'I can feel my thigh bone!' The other children started to investigate their own bodies and started to ask the pedagogue about the other bones they had found: 'Where's this one from? Have I got that kind of bone too?' The children asked what had killed the bird and scattered the bones in the forest. The pedagogue talked about the other animals in the forest and that it was likely that it had been a fox that had killed the bird for food. In the kindergarten there are stuffed animals, a fox, a badger, different birds and others. Most of these animals the children rarely see, but they see their tracks and know about their habits. The pedagogue and children put all the bones they had found into a bag to take back to the kindergarten for closer inspection.

## Work in partnership together with parents

Forming a partnership with parents is an important part of the pedagogue's role. Working together with parents supports the children in their care and the family as a whole. Working with parents includes a number of aspects:

- Being an adviser to parents.
- Giving information about a child's development.
- Facilitating social/information sessions.
- Working with the parent board of governors.

Advising parents has become an increasing part of the pedagogue's role, as many are asked to help parents solve problems they have with child upbringing, health, housing and divorce issues. Many modern-day parents, though well-educated, have fears about 'doing the right thing', and trust the pedagogue's support. For many parents, talking to the pedagogue can help them to solve problems themselves.

**Figure 3.3  Children inspecting bones**

The big uncertainty parents have can be relieved if the pedagogues help parents to find the answer themselves. And parents listen to the pedagogues because in their eyes they are qualified partners in their child's development and have real value. Parents in Denmark, and in Scandinavia generally, have a confidence in pedagogues that is quite exceptional. 'Frontline soldiers' – pedagogues, nurses and teachers – are best qualified to advise parents (Jensen 2005: 13).

Pedagogues give parents information about their children's progress and development in a number of ways – verbally as the children are collected from the setting; through writing the day's activities and highlights each day on the white board by the cloakroom; in formal meetings to discuss the child's language and general development; and through the children's own books. Each child has their own book that starts when they begin their time in the kindergarten. It is written in by the pedagogues and the children take it home for the parents to write in; the children also draw pictures in the book. The children really value 'their' book and often get it off the shelf to look through.

Because many parents are working outside the home, the pedagogues arrange social and information sessions for the parents to participate in. These can be coffee mornings or afternoons, guest speaker evenings, parents' evenings, a summer party for those whose children are leaving to start school, a working weekend day and a Christmas party.

By law, each early years setting (and local authority childminder cluster) has a board of governors that is primarily made up of parents; there is one staff representative and the leader of the setting acts as secretary (but with no voting rights). The law states that the board must set the principles for the setting's work and a budget that follows the local authority's framework and goals. It also states that the board has a right to be involved in interviews and the employment of staff, including that of the leader of the setting.

## Key points

1    Danish pedagogy stems from the child-centred and holistic beliefs of Froebel and Montessori, and the social, political and cultural background of the country.
2    Pedagogy involves the establishment of different types of social life, educations and environments based on, and supported by, specific norms and values.

3   The formal training of pedagogues began in the late 1800s for those working with young children.

4   In 1970 there were three separate training routes for those working in: kindergartens and day nurseries; out-of-school centres; and institutions for children, young people and adults with special needs, and those experiencing social difficulties.

5   In 1990 the three separate types of training were amalgamated into one general education.

6   In 2001 a new qualification of professional bachelor for pedagogues was introduced.

7   A critical evaluation of pedagogue training in 2003 led to a more centralised professional higher education system and a new specialist training programme.

8   The present-day training of pedagogues demands that students specialise in children and young people, people with special needs, or people with social difficulties.

9   The pedagogue's role in early years settings includes creating a safe environment for children, being a role model, and supporting children's social and emotional development.

10  Forming partnerships with parents is an important part of the pedagogue's role.

## Reflections on practice

1   Child-centred and - approaches to learning:
    - Do you consider your practice to be child-centred and holistic?
    - In what ways can child-centred and holistic approaches to learning be seen?

2   Supporting children's social and emotional development:
    - In which ways do you support children's social and emotional development?
    - How can empathy and an understanding of others be fostered?

3   Training:
    - What is/was the content of your training?
    - Does/has your training give(n) you the pedagogical tools you feel you need to work outdoors with children?

■ Can you identify any further training you need to be more pedagogical in your practice outdoors?

4 Roles:
■ How would you describe your role?
■ In what ways can the practitioner be a role model to children outdoors?

5 Working with parents:
■ What is your relationship to the parents of the children in your care?
■ How do you support parents' anxieties and questions about child upbringing?
■ Do you have opportunities to be with parents in social situations?

## References

Bayer, M., Christensen, B., Helweg, D., Hirsbo, H., Poulsen, A. and Siegfredsen, K. (1994) *Seks I Een: Ny Undervisningsformer.* [Six in One: New Teaching Methods]. Herning: Systime.

*Børne og Unge.* Newsletter. 13/12/2014. *Danskere elsker daginstitutioner.* [Danes love daycare settings].

Jensen, J. J. (2005) *Forældressamarbejde; Støttepædagog til Mor og Far.* [Working with Parents; Support Pedagogue to Mother and Father]. Copenhagen: Børne og Unge.

Sigsgaard, J. (1978) *Folkebørnehave og Socialpædagogik.* [The People's Kindergarten and Social Pedagogy]. Copenhagen: Børne og Unge.

Williams-Siegfredsen, J. (2007) 'Developing pedagogically appropriate practice'. In Austin, R. (ed.). *Letting the Outside In: Developing Teaching and Learning Beyond the Early Years Classroom.* London: Trentham.

# 4 The learning environment

This chapter looks at what is meant by the term 'learning environment' in the Danish Forest School Approach and illustrates the importance of understanding the relationships between the children and adults and the physical space they are in, the pedagogical goals set and the activities being carried out. They are all contributory factors in the construction of a learning environment. The layout of a typical early years setting – indoor and outdoor environments – is described. Risk and challenge are discussed, looking at: the pedagogue's role; first-hand experiences; risk management; parental attitudes; and what happens if an accident occurs.

## Where is the learning environment?

In Denmark the term 'learning environment' means wherever we are – inside or outside. It is the interactions between the pedagogical goals, the participants (children and adults) and the physical space that construct a learning environment.

The pedagogical practice, the physical framework, and the organisation (layout, equipment, numbers of children and adults) determine the learning space. The indoor and outdoor environments should be seen as connected by the children and adults inhabiting the space and the context and purpose of the activities happening.

The Danish Centre for Educational Environments (DCUM) views the learning environment for children holistically, consisting of the physical, psychological and aesthetic elements.

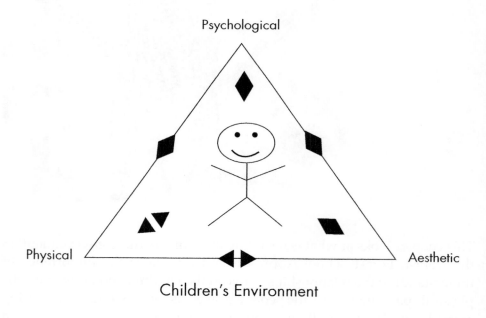

**Figure 4.1 The children's environment**

As shown in Figure 4.1, with the child in the centre, the environment is made up of:

- The physical element, including health and safety conditions, ergonomics, space, facilities and décor, make up the learning environment.
- The psychological element – how children thrive together, and with adults, and about the dynamic social skills that emerge in groups. A good psychological environment helps community, friendship, confidence, trust, care, participation, inclusiveness and challenges for a positive life.
- The aesthetic element – how the environment affects the children's daily life: whether they experience the environment as a nice place to be; this encourages their well-being and enthusiasm to learn (DCUM 2011).

The Danish Approach to the spaces children and pedagogues inhabit places high regard on the physical, psychological and aesthetic elements of the indoor and outdoor environments. This is partly because of societal beliefs, traditions and the training of pedagogues, and because many children spend a large part of their early lives in early years settings.

## The indoor environment

When entering an early years setting one feels welcome. There is an inviting entrance with candles burning (particularly during the long dark winter months of the year). Many settings now have digital intranet systems for the parents to register when their child arrives and leaves. Using their smart phones and computers, parents can also send and receive messages from the setting. For smaller settings, a paper register is still used because digital systems are expensive.

In all settings, the parents don't just 'drop off' their children, they take time to go into the setting and chat with the pedagogues and other parents.

### Uncluttered and functional

The indoor environment should be pleasing to the eye, well-kept and neat and tidy. The children and the pedagogues sharing the space need to be able to go about their daily tasks and play in an environment that enables them to move freely and independently. The children need to know where to find the things they want to use, and the pedagogues and children should share the responsibility of keeping things in order.

The classrooms have differentiated areas for different kinds of play and activities, such as an area where children can have space for floor games, another where they can have art and creative activities, and one where they can have peace and quiet. The resources and equipment in the room are easily accessible, and storage and furniture is arranged so that the children can work comfortably.

There are large cloakrooms where there is space for the children's belongings – coats, rain suits, thermal suits, wellington boots, thermal boots, slippers, a change of clothing, personal items – these must all be accommodated at different times of the year. Each child has their own space marked with a picture of themselves so they can easily find it. Visitors are often surprised by how big the cloakrooms are – often as big as the classrooms – but children need space to be able to put on and take off outdoor clothing independently.

There is a large kitchen where the pedagogues and children make early morning breakfast, bake the morning bread and prepare fruit for break times. There is a large refrigerator where the children keep their packed lunches. One side of the main working area in the kitchen has a raised floor so that the children can also be an active part of the food preparation process.

## Child-centred

The indoor environment is child-centred, with child-sized furniture and activities and pictures at their level. The environment takes into account the rhythms of the children's daily lives and has spaces for children who need a sleep time, to rest, to play and to socialise. The pedagogues see the environment as the child's space and, through their example, show a respect for people and things.

The cloakrooms and toilets are easily accessible to children so that they can be independent in their daily lives.

## Aesthetic

The indoor environment is welcoming for the children, a space they want to be in and where they feel safe. The children's work is attractively displayed, showing that the pedagogues value and respect their creations.

The areas are colourful and aesthetically pleasing to the eye. The use of candles has been mentioned a number of times and, again, in the classrooms and along the corridors there are night lights in glass containers to give a cosy atmosphere. Light is important, focusing on both natural and artificial lighting so that the spaces are lit for the purpose, either to be soothing or to be bright enough to enable children to see properly. Lighting can affect us physically, for example fluorescent lighting can cause headaches and tiredness, so the right kind of artificial lighting is considered essential for the children's and pedagogues' well-being.

Usually the kindergartens have compressed straw ceiling tiles which suppress noise and are environmentally friendly. Increasingly, environmentally efficient materials are being used in new kindergartens and when old kindergarten buildings are renovated.

## The outdoor environment

The importance of the four elements of air, fire, earth and water are evident in the outdoor environment. Spaces for different outdoor activities are provided so that children can have areas for physical activities and social activities to develop their all-round skills.

Wooden and natural resources are used predominately. Small wooden play houses and tepees are arranged so that children can play socially orientated games together. Living willow structures such as dens and tunnels are made by the pedagogues and children, which, when mature, give private spaces for the children to use. Bikes and go-carts are usually restricted to a certain area, so that children can play safely in other areas without the fear of being knocked over. Many of the bikes are two-wheelers without pedals so that the children can learn to balance. The go-carts are usually two-seaters, some with trailers, so that the children play cooperatively.

Mounds of grassed earth are provided for the children to climb up and slide down. These mounds provide children with excellent opportunities to develop their physical and sensory skills. Sensory swings are also available; these swings are large and round and develop children's kinaesthetic, vestibular and proprioceptive senses, which are essential for brain development and learning.

There are large digging pits filled with sand and earth so that the children can use their gross motor skills and have space to dig and use their imagination to construct roads, castles, etc. Children are fascinated by digging and spend a lot of time in these areas, either alone or with other children. Quite often the sand and earth are transported to another area, for example to the play house to create 'food'.

Real tools are provided so that the children can learn how to use them appropriately; child-sized wheelbarrows, spades and buckets are available and stored in an outdoor shed that is accessible to the children. The children learn how to use sharp knives together with the pedagogues outdoors. Children love to whittle sticks, it is seen as a social activity and one that has a calming effect; it relieves tension and stress and provides a time for the pedagogues and children to sit together and chat.

The fire pit is an essential feature of the outdoor environment. It pro vides warmth during the winter, a cosy place to sit and chat, an area to cook in and eat together, and children are fascinated by fire in an almost primeval way. The fire pit is usually made of two circles or squares of wooden sleepers or boulders; an inner circle or square for the fire and an outer circle or square that acts as a safety barrier between the children and the fire. Children know that they must not cross into the inner space. Quite often the fire pit has a wooden roof with a hole in the middle for the smoke to escape; this roof provides shelter in rainy, cold or windy weather.

Water is available for the children to use, and again they often transport it to other areas in their play.

Many of the kindergartens keep animals and, depending upon the size of the kindergarten and the outdoor space it has, these can range from large to small animals – hens, goats, rabbits, pigs, and horses are all popular. The pedagogues and the children look after and care for the animals together.

A pedagogue said about keeping Flemish Giant rabbits:

Large rabbits are soft and patient, when I put the rabbits by the children, they create closeness and intimacy. The can stroke them, read them a story – they help the children learn. In nature subjects we find out what they like to eat, what nutrients plants contain that are good for them. In maths we can measure and weigh them. In language we can find which words we can use to describe them – soft, sweet, grey, big, etc. The children also learn empathy in the way we treat animals.

## Risk and challenge

Risk and challenge are a part of everyday life as we are constantly assessing risks and taking challenges in order to live, learn and develop. In the Danish Forest School Approach, risk and challenge are vital elements; pedagogically, risk is seen as a part of the child's natural development and there can be negative consequences if children do not experience risk.

Risk and challenge offer a powerful medium for personal growth and development by building self-esteem and self-confidence, and in group situations they foster the development of trust, leadership and judgement. To take away risk denies the child the opportunity to learn how to tackle everyday challenges and problems. Only by experiencing risk and challenge does the child learn how to take care of themselves and others.

## No boundaries

Many nature kindergartens have no fences or formal boundaries, but they have invisible boundaries and waiting points that keep the children in a given area. The children learn about these demarcations when they start at the kindergarten and are reminded of them each day. The older children help the younger children (a nature kindergarten leader said that if one child went beyond the invisible boundary, there were 29 'policemen' on duty to tell him!)

In an unfenced environment it is important to always use the same demarcations and invisible boundaries, this way the children remember and respect them and they become cognisable.

> There is one special tree along the forest path. It marks the boundary: to this point and no further. The children are proud to show they are responsible. They run along the forest path, but at the 'waiting tree' they stop. No one goes on until everyone, children and adults, are gathered…. When the nursery was founded, a mark was scratched into the bark. It's now barely discernible but every day there is the ritual of finding the mark and remembering its significance.
>
> (Høndruphus website)

**Figure 4.2 The special 'waiting tree'**

## What is 'risky play' seen from children's, parent's, educator's and society's perspectives?

Sandseter (2010) acknowledges that risky play is a difficult concept to define, citing Adams (2001): 'The problem for those who seek to devise objective measures of risk is that people to varying degrees modify their level of vigilance and their exposure to danger in response to their subjective perception of risk' (Adams 2001: 13).

In this way we all make risk-versus-benefit decisions, and our decisions are based subjectively on our perceptions of the risk: balancing our own tendency to take risks, what we perceive as the rewards of taking risks, and the perceived dangers in the situation we, or others, have experienced. This balancing behaviour is what Adams calls the risk 'thermostat' (Sandseter 2010: 19).

### Children's perceptions of risky play

Children enjoy sliding, swinging, climbing and balancing in natural environments. Children differ in the amount, or extreme forms, of those activities, depending on their own levels of confidence and competence and their level of sensation-seeking and temperament. The sensation, or thrill, is offset by the feeling of fear – what Sansdeter calls 'scaryfunny' (Sandseter 2010). There are both potential 'rewards' and potential 'costs' involved in children engaged in risky play. Rewards can be positive experiences, excitement, fun and happiness. Children enjoy mastering new and challenging tasks. Other benefits of children's engagement in risky play are the 'lessons for life' that they unconsciously learn while handling risks. Children approach the world around them through play, they are driven by curiosity and a need for excitement, they rehearse handling real-life risky situations through risky play, and they discover what is safe and what is not (Sandseter 2010).

The 'costs' of risky play include injury and overwhelming fear. Serious injury in outdoor environments in Danish kindergartens is extremely rare; most injuries are minor cuts and scratches that require simple treatment at the kindergarten. Occasionally injury includes broken limbs or dental injury and the child requires treatment from their doctor, dentist or the hospital.

Only once I have had to drive to the hospital with a boy with a big injury. In 17 years.

And what was the injury?

It was a parent who drove over a foot of a kid in the carpark.

(Extract from SBS Dateline programme about Danish forest
kindergartens, *Kids-Gone-Wild* 2016)

There are no surveys that show that children have more accidents in nature kindergartens than other types of kindergarten, even though children play in surroundings that are not arranged according to health and safety guidelines (Ejbye-Ernst and Lysklett 2015: 22).

## Parental perceptions of risky play

Every childcare setting has a board of governors primarily consisting of parents. This board, together with the lead pedagogue, is responsible for the planning, organisation, activities and policies of the setting. As a part of this process they discuss health and safety, and risk and challenge issues, and are therefore aware of the activities the children participate in and the materials and equipment they use. Any parent who has concerns about their child's well-being can talk to parent board members about their worries, and these concerns can be taken up at a board meeting.

Most kindergartens have a 'working weekend day', which is a day when parents come to the setting to work alongside the pedagogues to make and repair outdoor resources. This means that they are well aware of the risks and challenges that their children experience in the outdoors. It is also a time when the pedagogues and parents can talk together about the importance of children developing their skills and competencies through taking risks and challenges.

Many Danish parents send their children to nature kindergartens because they fear that the 'virtual' world is taking over from the natural one.

As soon as they come home they want to play on the iPad. That worries us. So we try to encourage them to go outside and play more.

(parents explaining why they send their children to a forest
kindergarten on SBS Dateline programme *Kids-Gone-Wild* 2016)

Others in urban areas see nature kindergartens as essential for their children's health. Four-year-old Barbara was previously in an ordinary kindergarten in the city and had asthmatic bronchitis. Six months ago her parents moved her to a nature kindergarten. Barbara's mother said: 'Now she's never ill and is more self-assured, friendly and happy' (*Politiken* 23 August 2014).

Some mothers with children in nature kindergartens are nervous about accidents happening, even though they are happy for their children to be there:

> I must say I'm happy I'm not down here during the day because I'm a bit worried when he climbs to the top of a tree
>                                 (extract from SBS Dateline programme *Kids-Gone-Wild* 2016)

This mother's fear is consistent with an Australian study investigating mothers' beliefs about risk in outdoor play. The study found that while mothers overwhelmingly acknowledged the benefits of risky outdoor play, tension existed between their desire to provide opportunities for their children to safely engage in such play and overcoming their own fears and concerns about their children's safety (Little 2013: 24).

## Pedagogues' perception of risky play

A part of the practical training of pedagogues is about them understanding themselves, their strengths and fears and finding pedagogical ways of dealing with these. This applies particularly to those students who take the 'nature and outdoor life' elective subject during their training. These students participate in many outdoor and outward-bound activities that are physically and mentally challenging, such as kayaking, rappelling and bushcraft. These activities are aimed at developing their self-awareness, problem-solving abilities, cooperation and collaborative skills, and their fortitude.

The Danish phrase *tur efter evne* is used by pedagogues to describe their role with children in nature (Bentsen, Andkjær and Ejbye-Ernst 2009: 159). It means that they need to be aware of the challenges in nature, and what resources they and the children have to enable them to accomplish tasks and activities and feel a sense of achievement through them.

The pedagogue's role in nature with children demands two things:

■ Good planning.
■ Good observation.

Good planning and observation mean that the pedagogue needs to carefully think through the activity. They need to consider:

- What are the demands of the activity?
- What skills, competencies and resources does the activity demand the children have?
- The ages of the children and their physical abilities: is the activity one they will feel safe and motivated to do?
- Are there any physical resources they will need?

Good observation means that during the activity the pedagogue:

- Carefully watches the children's actions and emotions.
- Looks to see if all the children are feeling safe.
- Notices if there are any children who need extra help or encouragement.
- Decides whether they need to take a rest for a few minutes.

At the end of the activity the pedagogue talks to the children about what they have done and achieved and about the process of doing the activity. The pedagogue and children share the feel-good factor of accomplishment and can talk about tricky moments with new confidence and a feeling of self-esteem.

Studies into practitioners' perceptions of risky play indicate that there can be a difference in attitude related to their age, gender and personality (Sandseter 2010, 2014). Male practitioners scored higher on excitement-seeking scales than female practitioners; they had a more liberal attitude towards children's risky play and allowed children to engage in greater risky play than women. Practitioners are influenced by their own inclination to take risks and their perception of danger.

How the staff members in a pre-school respond and react to the children who engage in risk-taking play will thus function as a kind of filter for the actions that the children are able to actualise. In many incidents, the risk-taking decision will be made by the adult present in the situation.

(Sandseter 2010: 104)

## Cultural and societal perceptions of children's risk-taking

Attitudes to children's risk-taking vary across cultures. What is acceptable in one may be seen as unacceptable in another.

> Child development theories vary about the age at which a child is seen to be "responsible". In many parts of the world, age 5 to 7 years is an important time of transition in children's responsibilites and status in their community.
>
> (Rogoff 2003: 169)

It appears that between the ages of five to seven years, parents delegate (and children assume) responsibility for the care of younger children, for tending animals, for carrying out household chores and gathering materials for the upkeep of the family. The children also become responsible for their own social behaviour and the method of punishment for transgressions changes. Along with new responsibilities, there is the expectation that children between five and seven years begin to be teachable. Adults give practical training, expecting children to be able to imitate their example; children are taught social manners and inculcated in cultural traditions. Underlying these changes in teachability is the fact that at five to seven years children are considered to attain common sense or rationality (Rogoff 2003: 169).

Rogoff also states that we should not view this age of responsibility too rigidly, as it is strongly related to the sort of supports and constraints offered by the community.

> The ages of accomplishment are highly related to the opportunities children have to observe and participate in the activities and cultural values regarding development of particular skills.
>
> (Rogoff 2003: 170)

The Danish cultural and societal values of trust and independence, in addition to the fact that most children attending nature kindergartens are more physically and socially developed (through their interactions and activities in a more challenging outdoor environment), indicate that Danish children acquire responsibility at a younger age. Various studies over the past two decades illustrate that nature kindergarten children are more physically, socially and emotionally developed (Grahn *et al.* 1997; Lamprecht *et al.* 2004; Fjørtoft 2004). They are able to use real tools responsibly at the age of three to four. The pedagogue supports the children's risky play and encourages children to be an interactive part of risk assessment and responsibility.

## First-hand experiences

Children learn through first-hand, real-life experiences. The pedagogues offer children these experiences and build children's skills and competencies by allowing them to use real tools and materials in a genuine and purposeful way. Using real tools – knives, axes and saws – alongside the pedagogue encourages children's confidence and competence in a safe way. The pedagogically appropriate practice used to teach young children to use tools includes the following:

- First, the child watches the pedagogue using the tools and they talk about their actions and why safety when using tools is important.
- The next step is for the child to use the tools alongside the pedagogue.
- When the child has mastered using the tools and has demonstrated to the pedagogue that they are using the tools confidently and safely the pedagogue allows them to use the tools independently.

If we presuppose that children will harm themselves or others by using natural materials and tools we are disabling them, which has the effect of making them feel unsure, frightened and incompetent, and more likely to have an accident.

When climbing, young children generally only climb to a height that they are comfortable with, a height that poses a challenge to them but not one that is threatening. An environment with logs and balancing materials enables children to learn to climb and encourages them to gradually develop their confidence and competence to successfully climb higher – and to be able to climb down again, safely.

Learning about fire and its risks can only happen when children experience real fire. By sitting around the bonfire and feeling its heat with children and feeling its heat, the pedagogue can talk about the uses and benefits of fire, and the dangers of touching or getting too close to it.

**Figure 4.3 Using real tools with confidence**

## Risk management

The Danish Approach applies risk–benefit thinking to risk management (Bentsen, Andkjær and Ejbye-Ernst 2009: 160). The pedagogue needs to balance the risks that an area or activity has with the benefits to the children's learning and well-being that it offers. The pedagogue makes judgements about the reasonableness of risks and, together with colleagues and parents, must decide what an acceptable and unacceptable risk is.

The outdoor environment is unpredictable and the pedagogue has to take into account that the weather may change, equipment may not work or could break, or there could be an accident or a child suddenly becoming ill.

Children are also encouraged to make risk assessments themselves as the pedagogues see this as involving them actively in the process. By talking to the children they enable them to learn the importance of being safe and what judgements to make to assess risk before a challenge is taken.

Pedagogues must have up-to-date first-aid certificates and many kindergartens now offer children a short first-aid course. This has proved to be very popular with the children and the pedagogues feel that it helps the children be more responsible for themselves and those around them.

## Accidents

If an accident occurs in an indoor or outdoor environment it is recorded in an accident book. The pedagogue assesses the seriousness of the accident and takes appropriate action. If a child needs medical or dental treatment, the pedagogue contacts the parents and arranges to meet them at the child's doctor, dentist or the hospital. For minor accidents that do not require treatment, the pedagogue notes the incident in the accident book and talks to the parent when they come to collect the child.

Denmark, generally speaking, is not a litigious society and very rarely would a parent take legal action following a child having an accident. The pedagogue is seen as *bonus pater* (Latin for 'the good family father'), meaning that if they have cared for the child's well-being in a responsible manner and have not been negligent, then the incident is seen as accidental and the pedagogue not liable to court action.

Compensation is set under the Danish *Culpa* law, which states that any compensation should be reasonable and appropriate: large amounts of money cannot be awarded.

The partnership between pedagogues and parents is strong, and parents hold pedagogues in high regard and respect their professionalism and competence in looking after their children. Only if an accident was clearly caused by a pedagogue's incompetence and thoughtlessness would a parent consider legal action.

## Key points

1   The interactions between the pedagogical goals, the participants and the physical space construct a learning environment.

2   The physical, psychological and aesthetic elements of the environment are key features of the Danish Approach.
3   The indoor environment should be uncluttered and functional, child-centred and aesthetically pleasing.
4   The outdoor environment should provide spaces for different kinds of play to enable children to develop their skills in all areas of development.
5   Physical and sensory experiences are important for children's brain development and learning.
6   In the Danish Forest School Approach, allowing children to take risks and challenges is a vital element.
7   Experiencing risk and challenge allows the child to learn how to take care of themselves and others.
8   The pedagogue's role in the learning environment demands good planning and observation.
9   Children learn through first-hand, real-life experiences.
10  The Danish Approach applies risk–benefit thinking to risk management.

## Reflections on practice

1   The learning environment:
■   How would you describe the learning environment in your setting?
■   How do you include the physical, psychological and aesthetic elements in the environment?
■   In what ways do you make your environment a welcoming and safe place for children?

2   The indoor environment:
■   Is your indoor environment uncluttered so that the children and adults can work and play comfortably?
■   Is there a large enough space for children's outdoor clothing and footwear?
■   In what ways is the indoor environment child-centred?
■   Do you consider aesthetics an important element in your indoor environment?

3   The outdoor environment:
■   Do you provide different spaces outdoors for children to engage in?

■ Do you restrict the use of bikes to a certain area?
■ Is your outdoor area a challenging and motivating place for children?
■ What resources and activities do you provide for children's sensory development?

4 Risk and challenge:
■ How important do you consider risk and challenge in children's development?
■ Do your indoor and outdoor environments provide children with opportunities to learn how to tackle everyday challenges?
■ How do you see your role when planning activities outdoors?
■ Do you provide children with first-hand, real-life experiences?
■ Do you allow children to use real tools?

5 Parental attitudes:
■ What are the parent's attitudes to their children being outdoors?
■ How do you show parents the value of outdoor play?
■ Do the parents know how you care for their children and how you respond to any accidents?

## References

Adams, J. (2001) *Risk*. London: Routledge.

Bentsen, P., Andkjær, S. and Ejbye-Ernst, N. (2009) *Frilusftliv. Natur, Samfund og Pædagogik.* [Friluftliv. Nature, Society and Pedagogy]. Copenhagen: Munksgaard.

DCUM (Dansk Center for Undervisningsmiljø) [Danish Centre for Educational Environments]. (2011) *Børnemiljø* [Children's Environment]. www.dcum.dk. Accessed 20 January 2011.

Ejbye-Ernst, N. and Lysklett, O.B. (2015) *Er Naturen Farlig? Om børns leg i naturbørnehaver.* [Is Nature Dangerous? About play in nature kindergartens]. Akademisk Forlag (e-publication).

Fjørtoft, I. (2004) 'Landscape as playscape: The effects of natural environments on children's play and motor development'. *Children, Youth and Environments* 14 (2): 21–44.

Grahn, P., Mårtensson, E., Lindblad, B., Nilsson, P. and Ekman, A. (1997) *Ute På Dagis* [Outside in the Day Nursery]. Alnarp, Sweden: Förlag Movium.

Høndruphus: www.hoendruphus.dk. Accessed 11 February 2011 and 30 May 2016.

Lamprecht, L., Markmann, S., Tyberg, F. and Vilhelmsen, J. (2004) *Liv, Leg og Læring I Naturen* [Life, Play and Learning in Nature]. KID-Projekt report. Available from www.naturpaedagogik.dk/rapporter/kidprojektrap.pdf. Accessed 18 January 2011 and 30 May 2016.

Little, H. (2013) 'Mothers' beliefs about risk and risk-taking in children's outdoor play'. *Journal of Adventure Education and Outdoor Learning 15(1):* 24–39.

Politiken (2014) 'Forældre til børn I skovbørnehaver: Lad vores børn blive' ['Parents to children in nature kindergartens: Let our children stay']. *Politeken,* 23 August.

Rogoff, B. (2003) *The Cultural Nature of Human Development.* New York: Oxford University Press.

Sandseter, E.B.H. (2010) *Scaryfunny. A qualitative study of risky play among preschool children.* Thesis for the degree of Philosophiae Doctor, Norwegian University of Science and Technology, Trondheim, May 2010.

Sandseter, E.B.H. (2014) 'Early childhood education and care practitioners' perceptions of children's risky play; examining the influence of personality and gender'. *Early Child Development and Care 184(3):* 434–449.

SBS (2016) *Kids-Gone-Wild.* www.sbs.com.au/news/dateline/story/kids-gone-wild. Accessed 23 February 2016

# 5 | The Danish early years curriculum

This chapter looks at the Danish early years curriculum, the areas of learning, and the way pedagogues facilitate the learning processes. Connections between the early years curriculum and sensory development are discussed. In the final part of the chapter, the national appraisals and evaluations of the curriculum are outlined.

The curriculum for early years settings in Denmark became law in 2004 and every institution has to make an institutional curriculum plan that covers six areas of learning:

1   The child's all-round personal development.
2   Social development.
3   Language.
4   Body and movement.
5   Nature and natural phenomenon.
6   Cultural expression and values.

Within these six areas, the pedagogues should facilitate four learning processes: 'to be able', 'to experience', 'to enjoy' and 'to understand' (Hansen 2003: 17).

In order 'to be able' to develop physical skills children need opportunities to climb, jump, run, and cycle. These processes include the sensory, bodily, social and intellectual competencies that children develop through them. Children develop positive self-image by using the outdoor environment because they can 'test' themselves in the physical activities they participate in. They develop important self-regulatory skills by learning to take turns and follow routines.

'To experience' in nature means that children can feel wonderment in the outdoors, joy and happiness and the frightening, in the safe knowledge that others are around them.

'To enjoy' means that children, through nature, take pleasure in sensory experiences – the smells, sounds, tastes and touch that being in an outdoor environment brings. Sitting round a fire, feeling its warmth on a cold day, listening to the trees rustling in the wind, and tasting the pancakes made on the fire; all give pleasure and enjoyment that is part of the learning processes.

'To understand' means that the outdoor environment can be the natural arena where children can learn about some of the 'mysteries' of life-cycle processes; also ethics and morals can be discussed by the educators and children in this natural context. Finding a dead animal, for example, raises many discussions on life and death, and the fascination the next day at discovering that the animal has disappeared or been part-eaten, leads to a deeper understanding of the forces of nature and gives the children the possibility of talking about their feelings – sympathy, fear, etc.

Educators in Denmark believe that these four learning processes are crucial if a child is to develop the skills and competencies that come with being a whole person.

## The early years curriculum and sensory development

The starting point for a holistic approach to didactics and practice in the early years curriculum is sensory development and integration (Borre 2015: 209). For a young child, sensory experiences are not split into separate categories – touching, seeing, hearing, etc. Senses constitute a wholeness for the child in synthesis (Hansen 2003: 18). During the first seven years, a child learns to sense their body and the world around them and to be and move more effectively in that world.

Most of the activity in the first seven years of life is part of one process: the process of organising the sensations in the nervous system.

> As the child experiences sensations, he gradually learns to organise them within his brain and find out what they mean.
>
> (Ayres 1983: 13)

Young children need sensory stimulation in order for them to master their bodies and make sense of the world around them. By walking over uneven terrain in the forest, climbing, swinging, sliding and all the physical movements that they make, a child builds their sensory-motor foundations. Nature kindergartens use nature and the natural environment to implement the six areas of learning in the early years curriculum. In this way sensory-motor stimulation occurs in all six areas and not just the 'body and movement' area.

The pedagogues provide the right environment and activities to motivate children's sensory-motor stimulation and development. Through these stimuli the child develops responses to their sensory experiences. Before a child can make these adaptive responses they need to organise the sensations from their body and the environment.

> Nobody can make an adaptive response for the child; he must do it himself. Fortunately, children are designed to enjoy activities that challenge them to experience new sensations and develop new motor functions. It is fun to integrate sensations and form adaptive responses.
>
> (Ayres. 1983: 14)

If a child has poor sensory integration they can have difficulty in learning to read and write and can also have behaviour difficulties (Ayres 1983: 7).

There is no 'proof' that children in nature kindergartens have better sensory integration and will therefore be 'ready' to learn to read, write, etc. in school. However, research studies strongly indicate that these children have better concentration, better language development, better social skills and better brain function and memory (Dietrich *et al.* 2002; Fjørtoft 2004; Grahn *et al.* 1997; Hansen and Nielsen 2005; Pedersen 2005, Ejbye-Ernst 2014).

## Evaluation of the early years curriculum

Under the 2010 Day Care Act all early years settings are required to:

- Describe relevant teaching methods and activities undertaken to achieve the goals of the curriculum and show how it is evaluated.
- Show how their plan will be implemented for children with special needs.
- Show that the child's learning environment is an integral part of the whole curriculum and that the children have been actively involved in evaluations.
- Ensure that the head of the setting evaluates the curriculum and syllabus at least every two years and that the local education authority has approved them.
- Demonstrate that the head of the setting has ensured that the parent's board of governors is involved in the setting, evaluation and follow-up of the curriculum and syllabus.

*DCUM 2010 (Dansk Center for Undervisningsmiljø [Danish Centre for Educational Environments])*

An evaluation of what effect the early years curriculum has had on the pedagogical work of pedagogues and in building children's competencies, was made in 2012 by the Danish Evaluation Institute (EVA). The evaluation looked in particular at the five primary intentions of the early years curriculum law:

1 To contribute to strengthen children's learning and development.
2 To contribute to set focus on children with particular needs.
3 To contribute to more systematic methods of pedagogical work.
4 To contribute for greater transparency of communication and involvement with parents, local authorities and politicians.

5    To contribute to the strengthening of children's competencies in preparation for them starting school.

(EVA 2012: 9)

EVA's evaluation collected data by questionnaire from every municipality's pedagogical consultant and kindergarten leader throughout the country. It also made case studies in four municipalities, which consisted of interviews with municipality education department leaders, pedagogical consultants, kindergarten leaders and pedagogues. It also made an analysis of the kindergartens' curriculum documentation.

Based on this data, EVA evaluated the five primary intentions of the early years curriculum law. Briefly, the evaluation showed:

1    There was a strengthening of children's learning and development. The pedagogues were more reflective about their practice and there was more didactic thought given to the activities they performed with the children.
2    For children with particular needs it was found that the early years curriculum was not a useful tool for improvement. However, they found it was useful for focusing on how these children receive the best possible pedagogical framework.
3    There were mixed results regarding the early years curriculum's effect on pedagogues being more systematic in their work: 'Only some of the 15 curriculum plans analysed can be characterised as plans in the sense that they define different future activities in time and space, or describe a procedure for planning, implementation, documentation and evaluation' (EVA 2012: 10).
4    It was found that the early years curriculum had created a greater transparency and improved communication of the pedagogical content of their work with parents, local authority and politicians.
5    Has the early years pedagogy contributed to children being better prepared for school? Interestingly, half of the reception class teachers interviewed felt that fewer children today are 'ready' for school, compared with five to eight years ago. Children's language development was better, but their competencies within the areas of nature and natural phenomena, cultural expression and values, and in body and movement were not improved.

As written earlier, children who attend nature kindergartens have a lot of knowledge and experience about nature and natural phenomena and are better developed physically. This would indicate that *all* children need nature-kindergarten-type experiences to enable them to be 'ready' for school.

In 2014 a Consolidation Act was brought into force by the Danish government (UVM 2014). The purpose of this Act is to:

1   Promote the welfare, development and learning of children and young people through day-care, after-school, and club facilities, and other socio-pedagogic after-school facilities.
2   Provide families with flexibility and options as regards various types of facilities and subsidies so that, to the extent possible, families can plan family and working life according to their needs and wishes.
3   Prevent the vicious circle of deprivation and exclusion by making pedagogic measures an integral part of the local authority's overall offer to children and young people. Similarly, to offer preventative and supportive activities aimed at children and young people requiring special support, including children and young people with diminished mental or physical capacity.
4   Create coherence and continuity between facilities and make transitions between facilities coherent and age-appropriately challenging for them

(UVM 2014: 1)

The Act details the responsibilities of the local authorities, individual day-care settings, and a setting's board of governors.

Following the EVA evaluation report and the Consolidation Act, the Education Minister set up a Quality Forum for Day Care. On the 27 January 2016 the Ministry announced that a Quality Forum would be set up:

If all children will have the same possibilities for a good start to life, all those around children need to take the responsibility for the development of child minders and day-care settings. Therefore the Minister for Children, Education and Equality has set up a new Quality Forum for Day Care.

(UVM 2016a)

Subsequently, in March 2016 the minister announced that a Master Group was to be set up to 'strengthen the early years curriculum' (UVM 2016b). The announcement states that the early years curriculum has, since 2004, played a central role for pedagogues, but that evaluations have shown that there are some challenges. The Master Group will come up with some suggestions as to how the curriculum can be strengthened:

The Master Group will make a collective recommendation for a framework for the new early years curriculum. The framework will contain suggestions for a collective understanding of quality of learning in day care, offer of the curriculums themes, which learning objectives make the way to a good learning environment, and how the strengthened curriculum can support the evaluation culture in day care.

(UVM 2016b)

The Master Group initiative started in March 2016 and in October of that year they will present their recommendations for the framework to strengthen the curriculum to the Minister of Education. The Master Group's focus areas are:

- To develop a collective foundation of pedagogical values.
- To make an evaluation of the six areas of learning.
- To find ways that the curriculum can be better for vulnerable children and children from disadvantaged backgrounds.
- Strengthening partnership with parents.
- Strengthening children's competencies in preparation for them starting school.
- Strengthening the processes of evaluation in childcare settings – particularly reflective models of evaluation and assessment.

During the period, pedagogues, local education authority consultants, parents and children are invited to be an active part of the process by emailing the education ministry with their thoughts, ideas, comments, etc. These will be used in the Master Group's meetings and discussions (UVM 2016c).

## Key points

1 The Danish early years curriculum covers six areas of learning.
2 Pedagogues facilitate four learning processes to enable children's development.
3 The starting point for a holistic approach to didactics and practice in the early years curriculum is through sensory development and integration.
4 Young children need sensory stimulation in order for them to master their bodies and make sense of the world around them.

5   Nature kindergartens use nature and the natural environment to implement the six areas of learning in the curriculum.
6   Pedagogues provide the right environment and activities to motivate children's sensory-motor stimulation and development.
7   The Danish Evaluation Institute (EVA) evaluated the early years curriculum as generally effective, but there were areas for improvement.
8   The 2014 Consolidation Act for Day Care Facilities details the responsibilities of the local authorities, individual day-care settings and settings' board of governors.
9   In January 2016 the Education Minister set up a Quality Forum for Day Care.
10  In March 2016 the Education Minister set up a Master Group to strengthen the early years curriculum.

## Reflections on practice

1   The early years curriculum:
    ■ Should the areas of learning in an early years curriculum be subject- or experience-based?
    ■ To what extent should practitioners involve children in life-cycle processes?

2   The early years curriculum and sensory development:
    ■ How can practitioners set up outdoor areas to promote children's sensory development?
    ■ How can practitioners assess children's sensory integration?

3   Evaluation of the early years curriculum:
    ■ What evaluations have been made on your early years curriculum?
    ■ Who should be involved in making curriculum evaluations?

## References

Ayres, A. (1983) *Sensory Integration and the Child*. California: Western Psychological Services.
Borre, B. (2015) 'Krop, sanser og bevægelse I det pædagogiske arbejde' ['Body, senses and movement in pedagogical work']. In Checchin, D. (ed.). *Barndomspædagogik I Dagtilbud*. [Childhood Pedagogy in Child Care Facilities]. Copenhagen: Akademisk Förlag.

DCUM (Dansk Center for Undervisningsmiljø) [Danish Centre for Educational Environments]. (2010) *Dagtilbudloven i uddrag med ændringer gældende fra 01. juli 2010.* [Daycare Act extract with changes in force from 1 July 2010]. www.dcum.dk. Accessed 22 September 2010.

Dietrich, K., Jacobsen, C., Mygind, E. and Stelter, R. (2002) 'A weekly nature day in a Danish "Folkeskole". An educational setting'. In Dietrich, K. (ed.). *Socialisation and the Social Change in Movement Culture and Sport.* Institute of Exercise and Sport Sciences: University of Copenhagen.

Ejbye-Ernst, N. (2014) *God Praksis? Pædagogers formidling af naturen for børn* [Good Practice? Pedagogues promotion of nature for children]. Copenhagen: Frilufts Rådet.

EVA (2012) *Læreplaner I Praksis. Daginstitutionernes arbejde med pædagogiske læreplaner* [Curriculum in Practice. Day care facilities work with the early years curriculum]. Copenhagen: EVA.

Fjørtoft, I. (2004) 'Landscape as playscape: The effects of natural environments on children's play and motor development'. *Children, Youth and Environments 14 (2)* 2004, University of Colorado.

Grahn, P., Mårtensson, E., Lindblad, B., Nilsson, P. and Ekman, A. (1997) *Ute På Dagis* [Outside in the Day Nursery]. Alnarp Sweden: Förlag Movium.

Hansen, K.B. and Nielsen, T.S. (2005) *Natur of Grønne Områder Forebygger Stress* [Nature and Green Environments Prevent Stress]. Available from Skov og Landskab, Rolighedsvej 23, 1958 Frederiksberg C, Denmark.

Hansen, M. (2003) 'Kolbøtter, Kundskaber og magi' ['Somersaults, Knowledge and Magic']. In Christiansen, J., Hyllested, T., Nielsen, S., Paulsen, A. and Petersen, B. (eds). (2003) *Børn og Natur – Hvorfor og Hvordan?* [Children and Nature – Why and How?] Copenhagen: CVU-Sealand.

Pedersen, B. (2005) *Børn og Motion* [Children and Exercise]. Denmark: Nyt Nordisk Förlag.

UVM. (2014) *Consolidation Act on Day-Care, After-School and Club Facilities, etc. for Children and Young People (Day-Care Facilities Act).* Available from www.eng.uvm.dk/Daycare/About-Day-care, 22 October 2014.

UVM. (2016a) *De yngste børn I centrum for nyt kvalitetsforum for Dagtilbud* [The youngest children in the centre for new quality forum for day care facilities]. UVM Newsletter, 27 January 2016.

UVM. (2016b) *Mastergruppe skal give forslag til styrkede læreplaner* [Master Group will give recommendations to strengthen the early years curriculum]. UVM Newsletter, 7 March 2016.

UVM. (2016c) *Interview med Andreas Rasch-Christensen om styrkede læreplane* [Interview with Andreas Rasch-Christensen about strengthening the early years curriculum]. UVM Newsletter, 21 May 2016

# 6 Organisation of Danish early years settings

This chapter provides the background to the organisation of Danish early years settings, from Froebel's influence to today's pedagogical practice. The different types of provision are discussed, outlining local authority and private provision and the fees for these services. The staff organisation and the yearly and daily patterns are outlined and three examples are given to illustrate the organisational practices of three different settings: a nature kindergarten set in a forest, a nature kindergarten set by water, and an age-integrated private childcare centre in the suburbs of a town. National language assessment and early-intervention screening is described. Finally, methods of evaluation and documentation are given in detail.

## Background

The Danish Approach to using the outdoors as a part of the pedagogy of early years settings has its roots in the work of Friedrich Froebel. Froebel inspired Danish pedagogues to start a kindergarten system that included natural environments and opportunities for young children to develop and learn outdoors. From this, a more child-centred approach to children's learning and development evolved, leading to more humanistic beliefs within childcare and education. This led to what is referred to as 'reform pedagogy'. Reform pedagogy is based upon the individual child and the development of their independent and autonomous personality. Many of the ideals of reform pedagogy also affected other parts of Danish society in the political, social and economic areas leading to a democratic and, to a large extent, classless society.

Present-day pedagogy sees child upbringing and the relationships between the child, the family and society in a democratic and humanistic way. A survey conducted in 2009 by Copenhagen Council showed that the values parents and pedagogues feel are the most important that children learn in early years settings are:

- Self-worth.
- Independence.
- Consideration for others.
- Tolerance.

Furthermore, they felt that the most important experiences children should have in the settings are:

- Experiences of, and in, nature.
- Experiences with animals.
- Experience peace and tranquillity.

(Copenhagen Council 2009: 13–14)

## Types of provision

There is no single type of 'forest school' in Denmark. Each setting varies as to where it is situated – in rural, semi-rural or urban areas, and according to the people using them – pedagogues, children and parents: no two are the same. There are kindergartens that are situated in woodland and other nature environments and these are usually referred to as forest or nature kindergartens. There are approximately 500 forest or nature kindergartens and these form around 10 per cent of the day-care facilities in Denmark (Denmark.dk). In these kinds of settings the natural surroundings provide the starting point for activities inside and outside, for either the whole or a significant part of the day, every day, all year round. Sometimes things are discovered and investigated by the pedagogues and children in the natural surroundings outdoors and other times things may be brought inside the kindergarten for further investigation and discussion. Most of these wood and nature kindergartens are relatively small, with between 20 to 30 children and four or five pedagogues, although a few are much larger, with over 100 children.

Another common type of provision is kindergartens that have 'forest groups'. These are groups of children and pedagogues who go out of their setting for either part of the week or the whole week to a woodland area, often being bussed there. These groups usually have a permanent or semi-permanent shelter in the wood, although others – in urban areas where woodland is too far away – rent allotments in the town and develop these as their outdoor environment.

Many mainstream kindergartens just use the outdoor area that they have available, but even in these kindergartens the children will be outside for part of each day all year-round (Williams-Siegfredsen 2007: 63).

## Local authority provision and fees

Under Danish law, local authorities have to provide a childcare place for every child from six months of age.

There are four types of early years care that are provided by the local authorities:

- Day nurseries, which take children from 26 weeks to three years of age. These nurseries are usually found in larger towns and cities and are open 50 weeks a year, offering fulltime care.
- Kindergartens, taking children from three to six years of age. Some of these kindergartens are open for 50 weeks a year, others for slightly fewer.
- Age-integrated nurseries, taking children from three months to six years and usually open 50 weeks a year.

- Childminders, taking children from three months to three years. Local authority childminders are usually clustered into groups of four or five in a local area and offer parents fulltime child care for 50 or more weeks a year.

## Fees per year

Local authorities pay 70 per cent of childcare costs and parents pay 30 per cent. For each child aged six months to three years, settings receive 31,470.00 Danish Kroner from the parents. The parents' amount is based upon their income level, and is also less for subsequent siblings using the same setting.

For each child aged three to six years, settings receive 17,281.00 Danish Kroner from the parents. Again the parental contribution is based upon their income level and is cheaper for subsequent siblings using the same setting.

## Private provision

Private provision of childcare and early years education is a relatively new phenomenon in Denmark. A law passed by Parliament in 2005 made private provision possible. Private kindergartens and childminders have to be approved by the local authority and they must follow the authority's directives and policies. Generally, private kindergartens are open all year-round and many offer longer daily opening hours.

## Fees per year

For each child aged six months to three years, private settings receive 95,190.00 Danish Kroner from the local authority and 46,080.00 from the parents.

For each child aged three to six years, the private setting receives 50,588.00 from the local authority and 30,492.00 from the parents. Again, fees are lower for subsequent siblings using the same setting.

## Language assessment and early-intervention screening

Since 2014 all kindergartens, organisation plans need to include making a language assessment and carrying out early-intervention screening on all children.

Under the Day-Care Facilities Act of 2014, all children aged three to five years must have a language assessment; this is carried out by the local education authority and, under the law, parents must be involved in the assessment. If a child is found to need language support, the local authority have to work with the kindergarten and parents in offering the best support for the child (UVM 2014).

Methods of early-intervention screening have been developed following a research project set up by the Danish Social Affairs Ministry in 2010–2012. The research looked into ways of strengthening the tracking systems of children who were not thriving, and the best way to respond to children's needs as early as possible in their lives (Viborg Municipality 2015).

Under the Day-Care Facilities Act of 2014, all children aged 0 to ten are required to have ongoing screening three times a year. Screening is carried out by the pedagogues, teachers and leaders in every kindergarten, day-care setting and school, and it is the leader of each setting's responsibility to ensure that parents are involved and that the results are given to the local authority for their involvement and possible action.

If, from an analysis of the screening, a child is seen to be thriving and developing normally, they are put in the 'green' area. If there are some concerns that a child is not thriving or developing, they are put in the 'yellow' area and the pedagogue and leader will keep a close eye on the situation. If there are strong concerns about a child's thriving and development, immediate action is taken and a multi-professional case conference, involving the parents, is arranged. The aim of the screening is to identify children who have particular needs and through intervention are able to move out of the 'yellow' and 'red' areas into the 'green' area of optimal thriving and development.

## Organisation of a nature kindergarten in the forest

Høndruphus Nature Kindergarten is situated in a thatched cottage set in a forest, 20 km from the nearest town. It was opened over 25 years ago by a group of parents and now has 25 children and four pedagogues.

The cottage dates from the 1700s and is compact, with an entrance that combines with two cloakroom areas, an open-plan kitchen and living area with a wood-burning stove, bathroom for the children and a bathroom for adults. In the living area there are tables and chairs, a cosy area with a sofa by the window, shelving units with books, activities, and a range of stuffed animals (birds, a fox, a badger and small rodents that can be found in the forest). There is also a 'wonder cabinet' full of artefacts that the children and pedagogues have found in the forest. Upstairs there is a small attic room used as a sleeping area for those children who need a sleep during the day.

The atmosphere is welcoming and one has a sense that the children see the kindergarten as a home-from-home. The pedagogues are warm and responsive to the children and their parents, giving each their time and attention in an unhurried and thoughtful manner.

Outdoors there is a large area that surrounds the cottage, which the children use freely and which has play structures, plants and animals. Beyond this immediate area is the forest. There is no fence between, instead the pedagogues give the children imaginary boundaries and the children accept these. In fact, the only fences are those surrounding the animals – two goats and two rabbits.

There is a large sand pit with logs of different heights that the children enjoy climbing and walking along. Beside the sand pit there is a store with sand toys and beside that a shed with larger equipment including bikes and wheelbarrows. Next to the sand pit there is also a wooden water chute with a water tap beside it. The children spend many hours putting water into buckets and tipping it down the chute, or transporting water to the sand area. There is a large grassed area with long wooden tables and benches that are used for eating and playing and in the middle of this area is a tall flagpole where the children and pedagogues proudly hang their Green Flag. The Green Flag is part of an international award programme that recognises an education establishment's commitment to the environment.

Beside the cottage there is an old outbuilding used for equipment, and a workshop with tools and benches; the second floor has a small room that the lead pedagogue uses as an office. Behind the outbuilding there is another large area, part of which is used as the bike area and another part has swings, a slide down a natural bank, a wooden shelter and a sleeping shelter. Behind the cottage there is a garden area with a treehouse, planting area, bird tables and the oldest tree in the forest – a huge oak tree hundreds of years old that the pedagogues call 'the story tree' because it has seen so many things during its life that it has many stories to tell!

Each day groups of children go into the forest with a pedagogue, usually for two or three hours at a time. Sometimes they just walk round different parts of the forest, to notice any changes and just to be in the natural environment. Other times they go out with a purpose, for example den-making, mini-beast 'hunting', or collecting mushrooms. On these occasions they take a pull-along wagon with them with materials they may need – hand lenses, knives, paper and pencils for recording, and sometimes their lunch boxes and water if they are going to be away for longer periods.

> Children nowadays know so much about fantasy creatures but until they come to nursery here, they have no idea how small a fox really is... a lot smaller than a wolf! And in this real world of nature you can't just press the standby button or edit what's happening. We have to get out there, with our eyes and ears wide open. There will always be some animal inviting us to watch: a spider moving its eggs around. A dung beetle playing dead when it's alarmed (after a while we see it moving again). The toad that peed when it got a fright. Children see it all. Our job is to get down to a child's height to see it too, through a child's eyes. Nature is a gallery of beauty and at the same time, full of drama.
>
> (Description courtesy of Høndruphus' website, www.hoendruphus.dk)

## Yearly patterns

The kindergarten is open 47 weeks a year, with three weeks' holiday in July, one week at Christmas and five days at Easter.

Children are admitted into the kindergarten one month before their third birthday. When the child has been in the kindergarten for three months there is a meeting with the parents to discuss the child's language and general development assessment. This is a small kindergarten in a rural area so for children transferring to school in August of their sixth year arrangements need to made with up to six feeder schools to arrange meetings and visits that take place approximately three months before the summer holidays.

The pedagogues have made an illustrative diagram of their yearly pattern, called *årshul,* the year's wheel. The diagram shows what is happening each month, using the six themes of the early years curriculum, illustrating the kinds of activities that will be followed. The diagram hangs in the children's cloakroom so that parents can see it and know what their child is doing each month. The kindergarten also has an internal Facebook page and each day the pedagogues upload photographs and descriptions of what has been happening.

## Daily patterns

The kindergarten is open from 6.30 a.m. to 4.45 p.m. Monday to Thursday, and 6.30 a.m. to 4.30 p.m. on Fridays. From 6.30 to 8.00 a.m. children have breakfast, lunchtime is 11 a.m. and fruit and a drink is offered at 2 p.m. Every Monday and Friday all the pedagogues and children get together at 9 a.m. for about an hour. During this time they talk about news, stories the children want to tell, information the pedagogues want to tell the children, and so on. It is a special time for them to be together as a large family. Every Tuesday is the 'at home' day; all are around the kindergarten, inside and out and usually lunch is cooked over the fire outdoors. Every Wednesday and Thursday groups are out in the forest, for these days the children are age-grouped: three-year-olds, four-year-olds and five- and six-year-olds. Depending upon how many children are in each age group, there are one or two pedagogues with each group. The pedagogues are flexible in their daily planning to take advantage of new or unexpected events, for example, in Denmark it is traditional on a child's birthday for the parents to invite their child's group and a pedagogue home to celebrate. The season can also dictate activities, for example, when it's blueberry season, the children and pedagogues go into the forest to pick the fruit and take it back to the kinder-garten to make jam (not all the fruit gets back to the kindergarten, there are a lot of blue mouths after the harvest!).

## Evaluation and documentation

As has been said, each child has a language test and early-intervention screening after being in the kindergarten for three months. Depending on the results of these tests, they are followed up by interventions three times a year in conjunction with the local education authority's pedagogical consultant, parents and any other professional who may be involved. All documentation regarding this is digitally registered and kept on the authority's intranet site.

Høndruphus uses the SMTTE model to evaluate their activities (the SMTTE model is described in detail later in this chapter). These eval-uations are made in the staff meetings held during the last week of each month and they form the basis of the next month's planning.

Every child has their own file which is full of photographs, drawings and written descriptions of events the child has participated in – from the kindergarten and from home. The children value their files and often take them down from the shelf to look at, either alone or with friends, to talk about memories of special times. At the end of term before they start school, the pedagogues hold a special ceremony, together with the parents, and 'present' the file to the child together with a special gift to remind them of their time together. The gifts are taken from the nature around them – a special stone or leaf print, for example.

The year's wheel, as described earlier, also forms part of the documentation that the kindergarten has to produce and present to the local education authority to show how they are using the early years curriculum in their planning, activities and evaluations.

## Organisation of a nature kindergarten beside the fjord

Resen Day Care Nature Kindergarten opened in 1992 in an old scout hut beside Marienlyst beach on the Limfjord on the outskirts of a busy town. It has 32 children and four pedagogues; three qualified and one student. The unfenced area contains the old scout hut, a small Portakabin and a wood store. Surrounding these buildings are a large sand pit and wooden structures that have been carved by the lead pedagogue and parents for the children to play on. Long planks of wood have been arranged off the ground for the children to balance on. There is a wooden structure with a roof, which houses the fire pit, with benches around the sides. There are wooden poles that hammocks can be attached to and large sensory swings at the side. At the rear of the scout hut is a shelter with tools and a bench for children to do woodwork. The whole area is surrounded by trees, which the children call their forest and which are used for climbing and playing in. There are three wooden tepee structures in three different areas: one overlooking the fjord, one on a bank behind the scout hut with a view over the whole kindergarten, and one at the side of the trees with a view over fields. The tepees are fairly small, with just enough room for two children. The pedagogues have arranged them so that one or two children can have a quiet spot to sit in and look at the view.

Inside the scout hut there are two cloakrooms: one for the youngest children and one for the older children, and there are two children's toilets. The main area of the hut has a stone floor, a large wood-burning stove, tables and benches, a sofa, and a large refrigerator where the children keep their lunch boxes. There are shelves with books, activities and a small aquarium that the children use to home small aquatic animals and fish found in the fjord, so they can investigate them and learn their habits.

Beside the main area is a small kitchen with two small tables and chairs and a sofa. The kitchen also serves as the daily office for the pedagogues. On the wall there is an interactive-screen registering system where parents can click on their child's picture to register them when they arrive, and deregister them the same way when they collect them. Parents can download an intranet app on their smart phones and computers, so that if their child is ill, or they want to send a message to the pedagogues, they can do so and it will come up on the screen. Via this system the parents can also see photos that have been taken during the day of activities that the children have been doing. The pedagogues can also send messages and newsletters to the parents using the system.

The Portakabin contains a small classroom, which is used if groups of children want to investigate some natural phenomena. It is also used by the speech therapist and other professionals if they need to help any particular children who have additional needs. There is an adult toilet and a small multifunction room used by the pedagogues.

As stated, there are no fences around the kindergarten and it is in a public area with direct access to the fjord; the pedagogues have made imaginary boundaries and all children respect them.

## Yearly patterns

The kindergarten is open 50 weeks a year, with one-week holidays at Christmas and Easter.

Children are admitted into the kindergarten one month before their third birthday. The lead pedagogue has a formal meeting with new children's parents three months after they have started kindergarten and another three months before they start formal school. These meetings centre around the language test and early-intervention screening mentioned earlier. Once a month, parents are invited to the kindergarten for coffee and a chance to chat to the pedagogues and other parents. Each year they invite all the children's grandparents so they can see what their grandchildren do and join in activities. Once or twice a year the pedagogues and parents have a 'working Saturday' when they build and repair things in and around the kindergarten. It is also a social time for the pedagogues and parents to get together, and usually the day is concluded with cooking and eating round the camp fire.

Resen is part of a group of six kindergartens and all the children who are transferring to school are put together in one of the kindergartens three months before the end of the summer term.

Every year in September the municipality has a month-long theme of 'clean living'. Resen holds activity sessions around the fjord and its kindergarten about the theme and invites children from the municipality's kindergartens. In 2015, 280 children attended the activities.

Each winter they have a 'helping creatures through winter' project; they make bird feeders and other things to help the animals and insects over the cold season.

Twice a year the kindergarten is closed: once for staff training and once for yearly planning and evaluations.

## Daily patterns

The kindergarten is open from 6.30 a.m. to 5 p.m. Monday to Thursday, and 6.30 a.m. to 4 p.m. on Fridays. Children who arrive before 8 a.m. are offered breakfast, consisting of porridge, cornflakes, rye bread and milk. At 8.45 a.m. the children have fruit, before getting ready to go outdoors. From approximately 9 a.m. to 11.30 the children are outside, either in the immediate environment around the kindergarten or for a trip to the fjord, nearby lake or through the fields. Lunchtime is 11.30 when the children and pedagogues eat together and once a month they cook their lunch over the fire pit. At 2 p.m. the children have an afternoon snack of bread and fruit and vegetables; sometimes in the winter when it's very cold, the pedagogues make hot pasta and sauce or soup. After their snack the children remain outside around the kindergarten.

## Evaluation and documentation

As before, each child has a language test and early-intervention screening after being in the kindergarten for three months. Depending upon the results of these tests, they are followed up by interventions three times a year in conjunction with the local education authority's pedagogical consultant, parents and any other professional who may be involved. All documentation regarding this is digitally registered and kept on the authority's intranet site.

Resen uses the seven-sided model of evaluation (details of the seven-sided model are given later in this chapter). These evaluations are made in the monthly staff meetings and they form the basis of the next month's planning. After these meetings, the next month's plan is put on the digital intranet system so the parents can see what their child will be doing and what extras, such as types of clothing, they may need on certain days.

## Organisation of an age-integrated private childcare centre in the suburbs of a town

Tumlelunden is a private non-profit, age-integrated centre with 100 children aged three months to six years. Staffing consists of a lead pedagogue, 22 pedagogues and three kitchen staff. It opened in August 2012 in a large sports centre on the edge of town. The leader and parents converted the upstairs part of the sports centre, formally offices, to make a department for the youngest children (three months to three years) and four large rooms for the kindergarten department for children three to six years. A new purpose-built centre is due to open in 2017 adjacent to the sports centre.

**Figure 6.1 Bikes with child-carriers**

The department for the youngest children is split into three rooms for activities and eating. Leading off from one of the rooms is a large open-air veranda with a sand pit and outdoor activities; along the side of the veranda are the large prams where the children take their naps. It is a Danish tradition for young children to sleep outdoors during the day as it is the healthiest way and the children sleep more soundly in the fresh air. Outdoor sleep time is used all year-round, in all weathers – up to –20°C. The veranda has a canopy over it and the children use safety harnesses. There is always a pedagogue around the area when there are children sleeping. There is also a toilet and a changing room. The youngest children use the outdoor area around the centre and beyond. There are many different areas – a concrete area with bikes, the centre's own woodland area with trees, slides, fire pits and manmade tunnels. The outdoor possibilities extend over a huge area, so to make it possible for the youngest children to explore further there are several large motorised bikes with large child-carriers on the front. These carriers have harnesses so the children cannot fall out and there are safety helmets for them to wear. The pedagogues can also pack food and drink into the carriers alongside the children so they can ride along the forest path and have a picnic. The bikes are also used along the bike paths on the main roads around the town, so children get different kinds of experiences.

Indoors, the department for the kindergarten-aged children has four large rooms, three for different kinds of activities – large activities; small activities, arts and crafts; and one is used as a cloakroom that has space for all the children's clothing and a chest with a drawer for each child to keep their personal things in. In the cloakroom there is also an interactive screen-registering system so that parents can click on their child's picture when they arrive and click again when they leave. The system, similar to the one used at Resen Nature Kindergarten, also allows parents to use their smart phones to get information and photographs throughout the day. Lunchtime is taken in the sports centre's cafeteria area (the sports centre opens after 4 p.m.).

Outdoors there are many possibilities: the use of all the sports centre's facilities – football pitches and fields for other sports; plus their own woodland area with trees, slides, fire pits and manmade tunnels. At the rear of the centre is Liseborg plantation, over four square kilometres of woodland paradise. The children and pedagogues have made some basic bases in the plantation, which they use and the children are familiar with. There is no fence around the plantation, so the pedagogues have set imaginary boundaries and the children respect these.

## Yearly patterns

The centre is open all year round. Children are admitted into the youngest department from three months of age. Under the Danish Maternity Leave Act, mothers are entitled to take 14 weeks of maternity leave. During these first 14 weeks, the father (or co-parent) can take two consecutive weeks off as well. Afterwards, both parents are entitled to split 32 weeks of parental leave, which can be extended by another 14 weeks. According to the law, parents can receive a total of 52 weeks of paid leave per child from the government. The amount that the parents are entitled to is less than the amount of a full salary. However, many companies have an employee agreement in which they pay the full salary for a period of time (Danish Ministry of Employment 2009; The Local.dk 2015).

Children are admitted into the kindergarten one month before their third birthday; the majority of the children admitted have usually been in the youngest department of the centre, so there is a natural flow to their transition. Some children are from other settings and childminders and special arrangements are made for their introduction and transition.

There are two main projects each year that cover the six areas of the early years curriculum. The project themes are decided at the staff meetings and take their starting point from the children's interests, which the pedagogues have observed, and from where they see the most inclusive learning potential for all children. Alongside these main yearly projects, there are also shorter projects based on events such as festivals and global events, such as the one from 5 to 21 August 2016 on the Olympic Games.

All parents have formal meetings with the pedagogue for their child's group three months after they have started (for the kindergarten children this includes the language test and early-intervention screening mentioned earlier). There is also a yearly meeting between the parents and pedagogues to discuss their child's development. Parents are regularly invited for coffee and more informal talks with the pedagogues and other parents.

Being a large childcare centre with children from all over the town, transition to school takes a lot of time in the summer before the children start school – as many as 12 feeder schools are involved. Alongside the visits to the schools by the children and pedagogues, there are special activities for the children in the centre, such as cycling proficiency tests and other 'rites-of-passage' activities.

## Daily patterns

The centre is open from 6.30 a.m. to 5 p.m. Monday to Thursday, and 6.30 a.m. to 4 p.m. on Fridays. From 6.30 to 8 a.m. the children are offered breakfast, at 9 a.m. they have homemade bread and a drink, lunchtime is 11.30 a.m. and there are two afternoon snack times with fruit and vegetables at 2 and 4 p.m. The centre has its own kitchen and cooks who prepare all the food for all the children and pedagogues. The children do not bring packed lunches. The quality of food is important and this centre places high importance on the ingredients being of top quality and organic wherever possible.

All groups in both departments follow the same weekly pattern of one day in the sports hall, one or two days in the forest, one to two days in and around the childcare centre, and every Friday is an 'at home' day for everyone. On Fridays the groups can mix and the pedagogues can arrange activities across the age groups.

## Evaluation and documentation

Tumlelunden uses the SMTTE model to plan and evaluate its pedagogical work (an example of their SMTTE model is given later in this chapter).

The pedagogical documentation is seen at three levels: parents', children's and pedagogues'. At the parents' level, documentation is available through the website, the interactive intranet system, and in formal and informal meetings, to show the experiences and learning their children have been receiving. At the children's level, there is each child's book, along with displays and circle-time discussions with the children. At the pedagogues' level, documentation is used to ensure a continuous and systematic reflection of the innovative and developmental processes that the pedagogues initiate.

The pedagogues use the Marte Meo method to help them understand their relationships and communication with the children they work with. Marte Meo comes from the Latin phrase *mars martis,* meaning 'with one's own strength' and was developed by Maria Aarts in the Netherlands in 1987. Marte Meo is an interactive analysis method using video recordings to improve interactions between adults and children. The method has three stages: recording, analysis of the interactions recorded, and feedback.

> Considering human nature means creating a connection between events, thoughts and feelings. By understanding a child's initiative, we confirm their existence. Identity is created through interaction. The child learns about themselves from the way in which they are accepted, appreciated and loved. They react to events and situations through everyday life and through the reaction of adults and the environment in general. A child needs the help of adults to realise that there is a connection between events and feelings and in order to be able to transform events into words.
>
> (Roug 2002: 13)

One of the pedagogues at Tumlelunden is a trained Marte Meo therapist and works with the other pedagogues to help them improve their communication with the children and to be more aware of the importance of taking the child's strengths and capacities as a starting point.

## SMTTE and the seven-sided model of assessment and evaluation

Assessment and evaluation are an integral and ongoing pedagogical process in early years settings and the process should be viewed actively, interactively and reflectively.

Actively, because assessment and evaluation are a part of the whole cycle of events and the pedagogue is an active part of that cycle.

Interactively, because in most nature and forest kindergartens the pedagogues work in pairs or teams. The synergetic effect of making assessments and evaluations together with others – adults and children – can deepen the understanding of the learning taking place.

Reflectively, because for assessments and evaluations to have any relevant meaning the pedagogues (and, wherever possible, the children) need to reflect on the process: Was it the best way to do it? Did we achieve our goal(s)?

To make active, interactive and reflective assessments and evaluations, it is useful to have a model to base them on. Two of the most commonly used in early years settings are the SMTTE model and the seven-sided model:

## SMTTE model

SMTTE stands for Context (*sammenhæng*), Objective (*mål*), Action (*tiltag*), Evidence (*tegn*) and Evaluation (*evaluering*).

The SMTTE model is used as a tool that works towards common appreciation, description and assessment, because it:

■ Can be used to illustrate that you do what you say you will do.
■ Can make it simpler to plan and evaluate.
■ Helps develop one's own competencies during the process of completing it.
■ Can be used by individuals or groups.

Context:
■ What is the reason for choosing your objective?
■ Why is it important to use time and energy for this?
■ How does your objective relate to the children's needs?

Objective:
■ What is it you want to achieve? The objective should be realistic, relevant, understandable and positive.

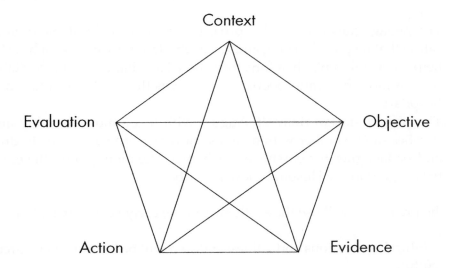

**Figure 6.2 The SMTTE model**

Action:
- What is your action plan?
- Who will be involved?
- When and for how long will you do this?

Evidence:
- How will you be able to see that you are working towards your objective?
- How will you document the pedagogical process?

Evaluation:
- From whom and how will you receive feedback during the process?
- How will you evaluate the process against the objective?

There follows an example of the SMTTE model in practice – translated from Tumlelunden's documentation.

## SMTTE model for the circus project – September to November 2016

### Context

- The project is for all children, six months to six years, each in their group.
- The pedagogues wanted this project to support a charitable organisation that inspires learning and raises children's awareness of how 'to help other children'. Therefore, they chose Hospital Clown (a charitable organisation that trains people to be clowns that visit sick children in hospital).
- The project starts Friday 26 August with a common assembly and finishes in November with a circus show performed by the children and pedagogues for parents and siblings. The money from the entry tickets goes to the Hospital Clown charity.

In the project we will use the six themes of the early years curriculum:

1 Cultural expressions and values: children will be introduced to circus culture.
2 Social development: to cooperate and listen to each other.

3   All-round personal development: self-worth and self-confidence – what I can do, what do I long for?
4   Language development: the use of body language, mime and increased vocabulary.
5   Body and movement: gross motor, fine motor, and sensory challenges and development.
6   Nature and natural phenomena: will be an inspirational source of content for the project's circus show.

## Objective

- Cultural expression and values:
  - That children are introduced to theatre and drama, as actors and audience.
  - Circus culture – what is a circus and what does it mean for me?
  - That children get an impression of, and knowledge of, what a circus artist is (for example, a clown).
  - That we make a Tumlelunden circus show.

- Social development:
  - Compromise and cooperation in each individual circus routine.
  - Waiting your turn – wait to receive help.
  - Giving space to others and their ideas.
  - Listening to each other.
  - Being able to laugh with each other, together, and not *at* each other.
  - Children's awareness about happiness and helping others.
  - That children's play and relationships mirror the community and the learning that the project gives.

- All-round personal development:
  - To strengthen children's courage and belief that 'I can, I desire'.
  - That children's self-worth and self-confidence strengthen so that the pleasure of being involved actively in a circus community is realised.
  - That children's fantasy and creativity is acknowledged.

- Language development:
  - Language acquisition, language use and improvements in written language.

- Mime – to be able to use mime relevantly and read others' mime and body language.
- That music and song are a natural part of the project.

- Body and movement:
  - Consciousness of what one can do, what one's body can do, and, not least, to listen to one's own boundaries.
  - To dare to challenge one's body in different circus routines.
  - To dare and, not least, learn to use one's body and face to dramatise.

- Nature and natural phenomena:
  - Nature and natural phenomena are to be involved in the creative processes.
  - To present to the children the history of circus and its development in connection to the animals and living creatures that may be part of a circus show.

- The adults' objectives:
  - That the adults have the courage to challenge themselves outside of their comfort zone.
  - To create happiness and laughter in the kindergarten.
  - That the whole of Tumlelunden can buzz with the common spirit, the common thread.
  - That the adults continue to participate in an engaged manner and to look for inspiration from each other.

### Evidence

- Cultural expression and values:
  - That drama and discussion around the circus project is part of the children's everyday play – on their own initiative.
  - That the children are curious and ask questions and are surprised at the things they are told.
  - That the children are keen, at their own level, to be a part of the community in the circus show.
  - That the children show curiosity and interest in the project: they talk about it, ask questions, and use aspects of circus in their play and everyday activities.

- That all groups work with, and buzz with, the circus – a lively feeling created from the youngest to the oldest.

- Social development:
  - That the children together, both with and without adults, are able to create circus routines.
  - That the children can wait without interruption.
  - That the children are more helpful to each other each day and take pleasure in this.
  - That the children turn to each other, across the groups, to get help and inspiration to develop an activity or a circus routine.

- All-round personal development:
  - That all children's development in participation increases: for example, daring to stand up during an assembly, or offering to take a role in a circus activity or show.
  - For the more reticent children, that we see they are happy and enthusiastic to be a part of the circus community.
  - We experience that the children laugh with each other and do not feel laughed *at*; that they can see the difference and not feel themselves teased every time someone laughs at what they do.

- Language development:
  - That circus language – dialect, mime, and increased vocabulary – is part of their everyday play.
  - That the children sing in their everyday play and maybe make up their own circus/silly rhymes.
  - That the children ask for songs and music.

- Body and movement:
  - That the children engage in the circus artists' events.
  - That children test themselves and their physical boundaries.

- Nature and natural phenomena:
  - That children collect materials from nature and the forest.
  - That the forest and natural phenomena are considered as potential elements of the circus show: for example, how could a frog be a part of a circus routine?
  - That nature is used as an extra space for circus play and circus workshops.

- The adults:
  - That the adults are role models for song, music and drama, and lead as guides so that the children learn that it is fun and not dangerous to create a circus.
  - That they laugh with each other every day.
  - That they share funny stories and experiences with each other.
  - That they produce displays to visibly and consciously illustrate the project.
  - That the adults use each other as sparring partners and sources of inspiration for the development of activities and productions.

### Action

- Trips to the library to look for books and music.
- Use of iPads, computers, etc. to look at and look for things about the circus.
- Assemblies take the circus as their starting point, planned by the pedagogues with contributions from the children.
- Children are inspired to create and help with their own small shows – for assemblies and in play.
- A creative space is made for exploring artistic aspects and making things related to the world of the circus.
- There is a writing workshop both for word cards and circus stories.
- Reading aloud, song and music are a natural part of the everyday activities, and also in assemblies.
- The hospital clown pays a visit.
- Props and accessories from the hospital clown are used in the project and show.
- The collection from the show goes to the Hospital Clown charity and is presented to them by the children.
- The adults ensure that the props and accessories are easily available for the children, so that they can practice the circus routines or just use them in play.
- The adults run activities across the groups, and watch for the children's different competencies and age-related development, so that the children can help and inspire each other.

## Evaluation

- Each group evaluates continuously in its monthly group meetings.
- There is a common evaluation in staff meetings, both for the baby room and the kindergarten. Partly to ensure the living thread between the groups and partly to run activities across the groups, and to make use of each other's different competencies for the benefit of the children.
- There is documentation, including photographs, etc., continuously put onto the digital intranet.
- After the project is completed, a committee is set up to make a collective evaluation using SMTTE.

## Seven-sided model

The seven-sided model originated from work carried out by two Norwegian education researchers (Hiim and Hippe 2007) who described the didactics between learning, experiences, understanding and action. The model is seen as an analytical tool to help practitioners understand the learning process and be as reflective as possible about their work.

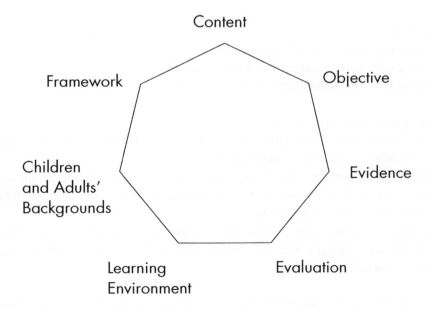

**Figure 6.3 The seven-sided model**

Content:
- The content means the action of the learning.
- The content should take its starting point from the child's all-round development and their emotional and creative needs.
- The content should illustrate the what, why and how of the activities and materials set by the practitioners.
- The content should show how the child's own level of development will be taken into account.

Objective:
- The objective should give the reasons for activities, for example, is it to develop a certain area of the children's development, or part of the curriculum?
- The objective should be realistic and doable.

Evidence:
- What kind of evidence will be produced – photographs, drawings, observations?
- How will the evidence be identified?
- Not all evidence is measurable and there needs to be room for 'soft' qualities to be meaningful.

Evaluation:
- How will the activities be evaluated?
- What methods of evaluation will be used?
- Who will be involved in the evaluations?

Learning environment/space:
- The learning environment is directly related to how we put into action and fulfil the objectives and content.
- The learning environment includes indoor and outdoor areas and should provide a variety of opportunities for children to have first-hand, meaningful experiences.
- The learning environment should allow for individual and group learning experiences and support each child's needs and their social and emotional well-being.

The adult's role in the learning space can be seen as being in three phases:
- First, the adult leads the way by introducing new experiences to the children.

- Second, the adult supports the children's learning alongside them.
- Third, the learning space can be child-led or initiated.

The children and adults' backgrounds:
- What are the physical, social and cultural backgrounds of the children and adults taking part?
- What particular strengths do the adults have, for example, a special interest in art or nature?

The framework:
- What concrete possibilities does the setting have to develop the learning processes, for example, is it close to woodland?
- What national and local laws and directives are there that will influence the activities?
- What is the geographical area, the buildings and the local area, and do these influence the activities?

Here is an example of the seven-sided model in practice (translated from Resen Nature Kindergarten's documentation). Using the early years curriculum theme 'nature and natural phenomena' they made a project around the theme of spiders.

### Objective
- To build an interest in and care for insects.
- To remove any possible fears children may have of spiders.
- To give an exciting experience with nature.

### Content
- Use the activity ideas from the Danish Outdoor Council:
  - Make an insect sucker.
  - Go on a spider hunt.
  - Make a trap.
  - See a web, catch a web and investigate a web.
  - Play the spider game.
- Make a display for parents.

### Framework
- Two adults and 16 children.
- Every Tuesday in September and October, in and around the kindergarten.

### Children and adult's background

- The adults' interest and desire to deepen understanding in the theme.
- The children's inquisitiveness and desire to experience nature.

### Evidence and documentation

- All the children gained a first-hand experience of spiders.
- No child was frightened.
- The children took the initiative catching spiders.
- On the information board outside our classroom we wrote about the theme and made a display so that parents could talk to their child about their experiences.
- We took photographs and quickly put them on the intranet so that the children could show their parents what they had seen; from this the children can build upon their experiences.

### Evaluation

- None of the children was frightened.
- The children began to understand what a spider is and what they do.

**Table 6.1 The learning environment and spaces**

|  | **Learning space 1** | **Learning space 2** | **Learning space 3** |
| --- | --- | --- | --- |
| The pedagogues' role in the learning spaces | We went close to the spiders to show the children that we were careful and that it wasn't dangerous. At the same time we talked about what we were doing so the children learned what things were. | We showed wonder and surprise together with the children when we caught spiders and investigated the webs. | The children went close to the spiders and touched them and enjoyed showing us what they did alone. |
|  | Adult-led learning | Adult-supported learning | Child-led/initiated learning |

- Some of the children showed skills they hadn't had (or had the chance to show) before, and they had the chance to try new things.
- We took lots of photographs which have been used again and again since for discussions about the experiences.

## Key points

1 The Danish Approach is based upon a belief that child upbringing and the relationships between the child, the family and society are democratic and humanistic.
2 Danish parents and pedagogues place high value in children learning the values of self-worth, independence, consideration for others and tolerance in early years settings.
3 Danish parents and pedagogues believe that children should have experiences of nature, animals, and peace and tranquillity.
4 Danish law stipulates that local authorities have to provide a childcare place for every child from six months of age.
5 Private provision is a relatively new phenomenon in Denmark.
6 The organisation of early years settings takes into account the staff and the yearly and daily patterns of the setting.
7 National language assessment and early-intervention screening became law in 2014.
8 All children have language assessments and screening at ages three and six.
9 Assessment and evaluation are an integral and ongoing pedagogical process.
10 Pedagogues use organisational models of reflective practice to assist them making their assessments and evaluations.

## Reflections on the Danish Forest School Approach

1 Relationships:
   - How do you view the relationships between the child, the family and society?
   - Are you aware of the special talents of your colleagues, and how do you value them?

2   Values:
    ■ What values do you believe are important for children to learn in early years settings?
    ■ In which ways can practitioners support children's independent learning?

3   Language and early-intervention assessment:
    ■ Why do you think it is important to assess children's language skills?
    ■ How can methods of early intervention help children thrive and develop?

4   Organisation:
    ■ Do your daily programmes allow time for practitioners to be together with children to develop their social skills?
    ■ Are the children split into age-related or age-integrated groups?
    ■ What are the pedagogical reasons for arranging children into groups?

5   Assessment and evaluation:
    ■ How do you view the processes of assessment and evaluation?
    ■ Do you use a model of assessment and evaluation to help you in your reflective processes?
    ■ Who is involved in making assessments and evaluations in your setting?

## References

Copenhagen Council. (2009) *Pedgogisk Perspektivsplan* [Pedagogical Perspectives Plan]. Københavns Kommune: Børne og Ungdoms forvaltingen.

Danish Ministry of Employment. (2009) *Consolidation Act on Entitlement to Leave and Benefits in the Event of Childbirth.* www.uk.bm.dk/en/legislation.aspx. Accessed 13 March 2016.

Denmark *Early Nature Lessons in Denmark's Forest Preschools.* www.denmark.dk/en/meet-the-danes/forest-preschools. Accessed 19 November 2015.

Hiim, H. and Hippe, H. (2007) *Læring Gennem Oplevelse, Forståelse og Handling* [Learning Through Experiences, Understanding and Action]. Copenhagen: Gylendal Nordisk Forlag.

Roug, P. (2002) *Marte Meo i Praksis. Bedre samspil ved egen kraft.* [Marte Meo in Practice. Better interaction with own strength]. Copenhagen: Nordisk Forlag.

The Local.dk. (2015) *Working in Denmark: Taking parental leave.* www.thelocal.dk/20150506/ working-in-denmark-maternity-and-parent-leave. Accessed 17 May 2016.

UVM. (2014) *Consolidation Act on Day-Care, After-School and Club Facilities, etc. for Children and Young People (Day-Care Facilities Act).* Available from www.eng.uvm.dk/Daycare/ About-Day-care. Accessed 22 October 2014.

Viborg Municipality. (2015) *TOPI Tidlig Opsporing og Indsats* [TOPI Early Tracking and Improvement]. www.kommune.viborg.dk/TOPI. Accessed 20 May 2016.

Williams-Siegfredsen, J. (2007) 'Developing Pedagogically Appropriate Practice'. In Austin, R. (ed). *Letting the Outside In: Developing Teaching and Learning Beyond the Early Years Classroom.* London: Trentham.

# 7 The future of the Danish Forest School Approach

This chapter looks at the future of the Danish Forest School Approach and outlines some of the facets that are a part of its success. The chapter uses research that supports the beneficial uses of the outdoors for children's development and learning. There are signs that indicate future trends in the Danish Forest School Approach from parents, local politicians and research perspectives.

## Parents

Many parents prefer small settings for their children. They see them as more child-centred and they feel that their child will thrive best in a small, closely connected community.

Some parents choose to send their children to kindergartens that offer particular experiences, such as forest kindergartens. These kindergartens are also usually small with around 20 to 30 children.

Unfortunately, because of stricter economic times, many local authorities are closing small settings and opening much larger ones to centralise and economise. Many parents would prefer to pay extra to keep the small settings open. This has led to a large increase in the number of private settings.

As mentioned in earlier chapters, private provision of childcare and early years education is a relatively new phenomenon in Denmark, and only became possible in 2005. Under the new law, if a local authority closes a kindergarten, the parents can start a private one. The parents pay an extra monthly fee to the kindergarten, and the local authority still has to pay a contribution as they did previously. The extra amount the parents pay varies and is set by the private kindergarten's parent board of governors. To give an example of parents' fees, Tumlelunden Kindergarten charges parents an extra 970 Danish Kroner per month. For this the parents benefit from all meals being included and the kindergarten is open all year round and is staffed with a higher proportion of qualified pedagogues.

There is an increase in the number of forest kindergartens in Denmark, many of them private, and this indicates that parents certainly want this kind of provision.

## Local politicians

Many municipalities are considering closing nature kindergartens due to demands on their budgets.

One Danish municipality announced in June 2016 that it was intending to close their nature kindergartens and stop kindergartens having forest groups, in a bid to save money. There was an outcry of protest from parents and the bid was overruled by local politicians. Of course, even with strong parent power, some closures are bound to happen because of changes in society that require extra funding in other care sectors, for example, Denmark has a growing elderly population.

## Research

Underpinning the Danish Forest School Approach is research indicating that using the outdoor environment and allowing children to be outdoors all year round is beneficial. It not only develops children's physical, cognitive, linguistic, social and emotional competencies, it also keeps them healthy. The research indicates that children who spend a significant amount of time outdoors each day:

1   Have better social skills:
    - Being outdoors has a positive effect on children's social relationships.
    - Children use their social experiences with each other; sharing, discussing, fantasising and constructing collective meanings and kinship.
    - Children's mastery of their surroundings happens in a social context.
    - Nature alleviates stress.

2   Are more attentive:
    - In the outdoors children are more attentive, have better powers of memory and concentrate on activities for longer periods.
    - Natural settings create opportunities for experiential and situated learning.
    - Nature's diversity gives the opportunity for various sensory experiences and can stimulate children's desire to investigate and experiment.

3   Have fewer infections and are healthier:
    - Being active outdoors develops vital muscle tone and increases weight-controlling hormones.
    - Babies being outdoors every day, all year-round, reduces the risk of developing allergies.

4   Have fewer conflicts:
   ■ Being outdoors helps children learn how to work together, follow rules and negotiate.

5   Have better brain function and memory:
   ■ Being active outdoors is essential for brain functioning.
   ■ Children remember things that interest them and they feel part of.

6   Have better language development:
   ■ Children use more complex language and construct longer sentences outdoors.

7   Learn vital life skills:
   ■ Using real-life, first-hand experiences with real tools develops children's competencies.
   ■ By taking risks and challenges outdoors children learn how to take care of themselves and others (Dietrich *et al.* 2002; Fjørtoft 2004; Grahn *et al.* 1997; Hansen and Nielsen 2005; Pedersen 2005).

More recent Danish research into how pedagogues promote nature in kindergartens has been made by Niels Ejbye-Ernst (2014). His findings show that:

■ Pedagogical work in nature affects children's strength, flexibility, co-ordination and concentration.
■ Pedagogical work in nature has a positive influence on children's general health, on their weight, on allergies and number of sick-days.
■ Nature is a stress-reducing realm, where children play for long periods with deep concentration.
■ Nature is a good place for risky play, which supports energetic exercise and can reduce accidents and phobias.
■ Nature is a realm that supports attention, self-confidence and fantasy.

Ejbye-Ernst also makes an interesting observation that most children spend approximately 10 to 15 hours per year outside in forests and other natural environments with their families, while children attending a nature kindergarten spend approximately 1,000 hours per year!

## Learning outdoors in mainstream schools

In early years practice, using the outdoors has been a normal part of settings and pedagogues' everyday work for many years, but for schools it is a relatively new phenomenon, starting around 15 years ago. The term used to describe what is known as a 'Forest School' in mainstream schools in Denmark is *udeskole*. *Udeskole* is a broad term referring to curriculum-based teaching on a regular basis in natural as well as cultural settings.

In 2000, two teachers from a school near Copenhagen started taking their third form (nine-year-olds) into a forest for an entire day once a week for their lessons. The teachers thought the children would learn different things than they could in the classroom and that it would be healthy and promote personal and social development. Over a three-year period a group of researchers from the Institute of Exercise and Sport Sciences at Copenhagen University investigated the project (Dietrich *et al*. 2002: 266). The research findings showed that being outdoors for their school lessons increased the pupils' energy and motivation for learning and had a positive effect on their social relationships. They also found that it increased their linguistic skills, as they used more inquiring and explorative language.

> *Udeskole* could be understood as 'outdoor schooling' or 'out-of-school-teaching'. *Udeskole* is becoming a widely used form of teaching in the Danish Folkeskole. A national survey of Danish schools shows that at least 14 per cent of schools practice *udeskole* to some extent, with about 60 classes practising *udeskole* once a week all year-round
>
> (www.teachout.ku.dk/english).

An exciting project called TEACHOUT began at Copenhagen University in 2013. The aim of the project is to obtain reliable evidence about the strengths and areas in need of further attention in *udeskole*. The main question is: do the alternative teaching practices of *udeskole* increase and improve children's physical activity, academic learning, social interaction and attitudes to school? And if so, how? Information about the project can be accessed at: www.teachout.ku.dk/english.

A recent UK study, funded by Natural England, published new evidence on the benefits of outdoor learning to pupils, teachers and schools. The study involved 125 schools, over 40,000 pupils and more than

2,000 teachers across the south west of England and was a four-year initiative to help school children experience the benefits of natural environments in their schooling. The key findings from the study were:

- 95 per cent of children surveyed said outdoor learning makes lessons more enjoyable.
- 90 per cent said they felt happier and healthier.
- 72 per cent said they got on better with others.
- 93 per cent of schools said outdoor learning improves pupils' social skills.
- 92 per cent of schools said it improves pupils' health and well-being and engages them with learning.
- 85 per cent of schools saw a positive impact on behaviour.
- 90 per cent of staff found outdoor learning to be useful for curriculum delivery.
- 72 per cent of schools surveyed found outdoor learning had a positive impact on teachers' delivery, health and well-being.
- 79 per cent of teachers said outdoor learning had a positive impact on their teaching practice and 69 per cent said it had a positive impact on their professional development.
- 72 per cent said outdoor learning improved their health and 69 per cent said it had a positive impact on their job satisfaction.

(Gov.UK 2016)

The future of the Danish Forest School Approach seems positive, both nationally and internationally. A growing interest in the benefits of children being outdoors from parents, politicians and researchers indicates that more forest kindergartens will be established, particularly in the new private sector.

From an environmental and health perspective, the benefits of children learning actively outdoors has positive effects on their well-being and develops their understanding of conservation and environmental issues. The Danish Outdoor Council ran a project from 2013–2015 called Education for Sustainable Development (*Uddannelse for Bæreddygtig Udvikling*). Green Shoots (*Grønne Spirer*) is the part of the council for young children between 0 and six years and they called their part of the project Sustainability at Child Height (*Bæredygtighed i børnehøjde*). It was aimed at childminders and pedagogues. Green Shoots arranged training and activity workshops throughout the country to involve and inspire childminders and pedagogues (Grønne Spirer 2015).

**Figure 7.1**

From an educational perspective, the benefits are being increasingly recognised by schools and more teaching and learning, like in the TEACH-OUT programme, is being carried out outside the classroom.

It is to be hoped that, despite the gloom of the economic crisis, the Approach will continue to thrive and develop.

## References

Dietrich, K., Jacobsen, C., Mygind, E. and Stelter, R. (2002) 'A weekly nature day in a Danish "Folkeskole". An educational setting'. In Dietrich, K. (ed.) *Socialisation and the Social Change in Movement Culture and Sport*. Institute of Exercise and Sport Sciences: University of Copenhagen.

Ejbye-Ernst, N. (2014) *God Praksis? Pædagogers formidling af naturen for børn* [Good Practice? Pedagogues promotion of nature for children]. Copenhagen: Frilufts Rådet.

Fjørtoft, I. (2004) 'Landscape as playscape: The effects of natural environments on children's play and motor development'. *Children, Youth and Environments 14 (2)* 2004, University of Colorado.

Gov.UK. 'England's largest outdoor learning project reveals children more motivated to learn when outdoors'. Press release published 14 July 2016. www.gov.uk/government/news/englands-largest-outdoor-learning-project-reveals-children-more-motivayed-to-learn-when-outdoors. Accessed 20 July 2016.

Grahn, P., Mårtensson, E., Lindblad, B., Nilsson, P. and Ekman, A. (1997) *Ute På Dagis* [Outside in the Day Nursery]. Alnarp Sweden: Förlag Movium.

Grønne Spirer (Green Shoots): Kryger, I., and Kardyb, D. (2015) *Bæredygtighed i Børnehøjde – at formidler miljø og bæredygtighed til førskolebørn* [Sustainablity at Child Height – to promote the environment and sustainability to preschool children]. Available from www.groennespirer.dk. Accessed 5 May 2016.

Hansen, K.B. and Nielsen, T.S. (2005) *Natur of Grønne Områder Forebygger Stress* ['Nature and Green Environments Prevent Stress']. Available from Skov og Landskab, Rolighedsvej 23, 1958 Frederiksberg C, Denmark.

Pedersen, B. (2005) *Børn og Motion* [Children and Exercise]. Denmark: Nyt Nordisk Förlag.

# Glossary

**Børnehave** – Kindergarten. In Danish *børne* means children and *have* means garden; the Danish title of børnehave is a translation of what Froebel called kindergarten: *kinder* is German for children and *garten* means garden.

**Folkebørnehave** Public kindergarten

**Folkeskole** – Mainstream school for children aged 6 to 16 years.

**Friluftliv** – Outdoor life.

**Naturbørnehave** – Nature kindergarten.

**Pedagogue** – A person who is trained to work with children, young people and adults in a variety of different settings.

**Pedagogy** – A holistic approach to care and education, including the body, mind, creativity and social identity of people. Linked with learning, health, and social and emotional well-being.

**Skovbørnehave** – Forest or woods kindergarten. In Danish *skov* can mean woodland or forest.

**Skovgruppe** – Forest or wood group. Usually used in urban kindergartens where they have a group of children who go out to the forest on a regular basis.

**Udeskole** – Outdoor schooling. Used in mainstream schools to signify school lessons that are taught outdoors.

**Vandrebørnehave** Wandering kindergarten

# Index